A Real
WHOLE LOT

A Real
WHOLE LOT

*A World War II Soldier's Love
Letters to His Wife*

JACQUELINE A. KANE

To order additional copies of this book, contact:
Xlibris
1-888-795-4274
www.Xlibris.com
Orders@Xlibris.com
739907

Table of Contents

Preface

I remember as a child playing in a closet where I would hide behind two large brown grocery bags. I was told these bags were full of letters from my father when he was in the Army. As I got older I never thought much about those letters and what had happened to them. We had moved twice and I assumed that they had been placed in another closet and I was not playing in closets any longer. In November 2015, my mother died. My father had died in 2007. With my mother's death, my brother, Philip, my sister, Kathy, and I had the task of clearing out my mother's last home. This meant going through her accumulation of family memorabilia. My mother believed in retaining copies of almost everything. I believe she felt that if one copy of something was good, one hundred was even better.

In going through the family archives, we found a bundle of about 200 letters on v-mail[1] and a dozen or so letters on paper. In talking with my sister, I found out that those bags of v-mail letters that I had hidden behind as a child had been thrown out by my maternal grandmother who came to live with us when I was eight years old. My mother came home one day and found the garbage men going through these bags and

---

[1] Victory Mail, more commonly known as V-Mail, operated during World War II to expedite mail service for American armed forces overseas. V-Mail used standardized stationery and microfilm processing to produce lighter, smaller cargo. It was used from June 15, 1942 to November 1, 1945. (Source: https://postalmuseum.si.edu/victorymail/introducing/timeline.html)

laughing at their contents. I can't imagine how my mother must have felt having her treasured letters thrown away without her permission. We don't know how these 200 plus letters survived that purge.

Having these letters transcribed has been very personal. Having the opportunity to have a glimpse of my parent's intense love for each other during the early years of their marriage as young adults has provided a different view of my parent's relationship. They were twenty-three and twenty-four years old when they were separated during most of their first 4 plus years of marriage.

Whenever these letters were mentioned to friends and family, it was suggested that they be published. I don't believe that there are any publications that reflect the feelings that my parents strove to communicate to each other during War World II and their separation from each other.

I am pleased to say that my mother's not so clearly expressed desire to have the family papers archived will come to fruition. Morgan State University has agreed to accept all of my parent's papers to add to the Beulah M. Davis Special Collections.

Jacqueline Anne Kane, Ph.D.

Jacqueline and Philip's oldest child

Introduction

Philip Gough Kane and Jacqueline Norris Jones Kane were born and raised in Baltimore, Maryland. Philip, who is referred in these letters as Phil, was the oldest of 12 children, 10 of whom survived childhood. Jacqueline, who is referred to as Jackie by friends and Jack by family, was the oldest of 5, 4 of whom survived childhood. Included in this introduction is a listing of their immediate family members. In these letters, Phil refers to Jacqueline by both names, since he met her in school and not through family.

Phil and Jack were raised poor. They both had to work to support themselves and contribute to their families. Phil was Catholic and Jack was Lutheran. Neither changed their religious affiliations but supported each other's religious practices and beliefs throughout their life together.

Phil and Jack attended Frederick Douglas Senior-Junior High School in Baltimore together. They were active in the Negro History Club and worked together on the high school newspaper, The Douglas Survey, were Jack became editor-in chief. They became high school sweethearts. Their regular date was going to the Enoch Pratt Free Library Branch on Broadway in East Baltimore. When Phil would bring Jack home, they would bring her mother's favorite treat, ice cream.

They were both behind in grades because Phil's parents kept him out of school until his brother was ready to go to school and they could go together. Jack, a chronic asthmatic throughout her life, had been so ill with asthma when she was 12 years old that she had to stay home for two years before resuming her education.

Both Philip and Jacqueline were grandchildren of people were enslaved on the Eastern Shore of Maryland. They were the first in their families to attend high school and graduate and then to go onto attend college and graduate. Although, Jack was accepted to Howard University with a scholarship, she elected to attend Coppin State College, a normal school/teachers college in Baltimore. In 1937, her mother and father had separated and her youngest brother, George, and sister, Cill, were living with their mother. They were eight and six years old respectively.

Phil elected to attend Morgan State College where he majored in English and graduated with honors. His senior year he participated in Walter Mack Jobs Award Contest sponsored by Pepsi Cola. His essay on "Why I Consider American Democracy Worth Saving" was one of the twelve winning finalists. He went to New York City and began working for Pepsi Cola as one of the first "Negro" salesperson to work in corporate America.

Jack upon obtaining her teaching certificate went to work as a licensed teacher with the Baltimore City Board of Education. She subsequently enrolled at Morgan State College where she graduate with a Bachelor of Science degree. At that time in Maryland there were limited opportunities for collegiate education because of segregation. The State of Maryland had a program, as did other states south of the Mason-Dixon Line[2] that would pay students expenses to go to institution in the north. Jack took advantage of this and applied and enrolled in a journalism program at New York University (NYU). As part of her preparation for her application to NYU and completing a writing course at Morgan, she kept a diary. Some selections from the diary are included amongst the letters transcribed since few of Jack's letters to Phil survived.

---

[2]   The Mason–Dixon line, also called the Mason and Dixon line or Mason's and Dixon's line, was surveyed between 1763 and 1767 by Charles Mason and Jeremiah Dixon in the resolution of a border dispute involving Maryland, Pennsylvania, and Delaware in Colonial America. It was used as the divider between North and South; freedom and slavery. (Source: http://news. nationalgeographic.com/news/2002/04/0410_020410_TVmasondixon.html)

Jack moved to New York City to attend NYU and Phil joined her. They remained in New York City living almost all of that time in the Bronx. They had three children: Jacqueline Anne, Philip Gough, Jr. and Katherine Maddox. They had four grandchildren and at the time of this writing two great grandchildren.

Time line for Philip Gough Kane and Jacqueline Norris Jones Kane 1937 - 1946

June 21, 1937   Phil and Jack graduated from Douglas High School, Baltimore, MD.

June 9, 1940   Jack graduated from the Coppin State College, then a Normal School/Teachers College, now Coppin State University

September 1940 to September 1945   Jack was a licensed teacher with the Baltimore City Board of Education

June 9, 1941   Phil graduated with a Bachelor of Arts with an English major from Morgan State College, now Morgan State University

Phil's Yearbook Picture

June 14, 1941	Phil and Jack Married
June 23, 1941	Phil traveled to New York City as one of 12 Finalists for Walter Mack Jobs Award Contest

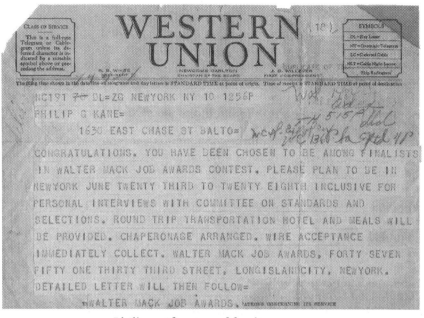

Phil's notification of finalist status.

July 1, 1941   Phil began working for Pepsi Cola.

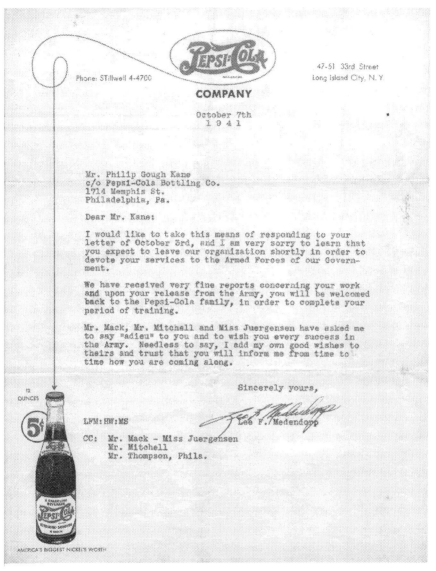

Pepsi Cola's acceptance of Phil's resignation

October 13, 1941   Phil enlisted into the Army of the United States

Phil's Enlistment Picture
Photographs by South East Army Air Forces Training Center

Induction Station No. 6

Baltimore, Md.   OCT 13 1941
(Induction Station)   (Date)

This is to advise you that

Philip G. Kane,   33,068,303   has been
(Name)   (Army Serial No., if accepted)

*accepted for active military service and sent to   Reception Center
(Reception Center, Replacement Center, or other installation)

at   FT. GEO. G. MEADE, MD.
(Post Office address)

where he probably will remain for a period of not to exceed 3 or 4 days. Upon leaving for his final
destination, you will be advised of his future mailing address.

*rejected for active military service and returned to his home.

This card to be made out and mailed at Induction Station at time of transfer therefrom.
*Strike out clause not applicable.

W. D., A. G. O. Form No. 202
March 15, 1941
                                    16—18304   U. S. GOVERNMENT PRINTING OFFICE

Notice sent to Jack about Phil's Enlistment

| March 1, 1942 | Phil promoted to Sergeant |
| September, 1942 | Phil promoted to Staff Sergeant at Columbus, Mississippi Army Flying School. Phil also served as an acting First Sergeant. |

Columbus Army Flying School

Columbus Mississippi

S/Sgt Philip G. Kane
831st QM (Trk) CO.

having satisfactorily completed the

prescribed Post Schools Course in

ADMINISTRATION
(Advanced)

is awarded this

Certificate of Proficiency

Wm. A. ECKERT, Jr.
1st Lieut., AAF
Post Schools Officer

L. C. MALLORY
Colonel AAF
Commanding

Phil and Jack in Mississippi

Jack in Mississippi

Phil's Staff Sargeant Picture
Photographs by South East Army Air Forces Training Center

January 6, 1943   Phil graduated in Class II Army Administrative
School Office Candidate School No. 1, held at North
Dakota Agricultural College, Fargo, North Dakota
and was commissioned as Second Lieutenant in the
Army of the United State. According to a January
2, 1943 article in the Baltimore Afro-American Phil
was one of four "colored" in the first graduating class.

Inscribed on the back: Background – the Administration Building.
Post Office is in the basement. How do you like the pose?

November 1944	Phil now have rank of First Lieutenant. The specific date of promotion unknown.
June 4, 1945	Jack graduated with a Bachelor of Science from then Morgan State College, now Morgan State University
September 1945	Jack moved to 128 West 138th Street in New York City and enrolled at New York University, School of Commerce, Accounts and Finance in the journalism program. She worked for $29.00 six days a week at Woolworth's Five and Dime on 125th Street.
November 27 1945	Phil began his terminal leave and joins Jack in NYC. By this time Phil had been promoted to the rank of Captain. The specific date of the promotion unknown.
April 13, 1946	Phil discharged from the Army of the United States

Phil served in the Rome ARNO. Southern France and Rhineland Campaigns. He was stationed in Algiers, Algeria and Marseille, France while stationed overseas in Europe and Mediterranean. Phil served as an adjutant for the various echelons of the Army Administration OCS. While in Marseille, he was a trial judge advocate and junior member of General Courts Martial.

Phil's Family Members

Siblings listed in birth order with married names

Philip Morton Kane (father)

Mary Priscilla Gough Kane (mother)

Philip Gough Kane

John Henry Kane aka Big George

James Albert Kane

Mary Clementine Kane

Agnes Emma Kane Callum referred to by either first or middle name

Thomas Merton Kane referred to as Merton

Howard Aloysius Kane aka Allie

Michael Ralph Kane

Mary Madeline Kane Byers aka Mattie

Edna Martina Kane Aiden

Jack's Family Members

Siblings listed in birth order with married names

George Jones (father)

Lucinda Maddox Jones (mother)

Jacqueline Norris Jones

Philip Jones aka Phil

George Maddox Jones Muhammed

Winifred Priscilla Jones Veazy aka Cill

Jack and her siblings, Left to right: Phil, Cill, George, and Jack

Letters and Diary Exceprts

15 January 1943

My dearest love,

Few more lines to add to the rest, that's getting to be a favorite expression, is it not?

Sweetheart, I hope you all quite well in every respect and that there is not a thing worrying you in the least.

Sweets, I'm per usual. Can't complain, dearest. I'm still being kept busy. You know that I am because my letters don't show it, do they?

Honey, I'm sorry that I can't seem to write more than I do, but I shall write more than I do. Your old man is slipping, isn't he? I'll make it up, dearest.

Keep sweet, love. I'll always be yours forever, Jackie.

Your husband,
Phil

P.S. Dearest, I love you—"a real whole lot."

Wednesday, 6:30 p.m.
February 17, 1943

My beloved wife,

I am starting your letter here in class. We have to go to class every Wednesday night for two hours—6:30 p.m. to 8:30 p.m.

I am going to write you all during class—if I don't, I will certainly go to sleep. Some guy is going to tell me something about court-martials. More time thrown away. That's all it is. They fooled us and showed us a film on why it is so essential that persons concerned with the government keep their mouths shut concerning military matters and operations. It was interesting, and as a result could not permit me to finish your letter. So I am starting it right here.

I hope this will be one of those long letters. One like I used to write.

The weather has improved considerably, to the place where I can get along with it. I have, however, developed a sore throat. I will get some Listerine and gargle with it; that should improve it. Otherwise, I'm doing all right.

Darling, I do hope that everything is coming along quite well. That you're resting up for this weekend and all that sort of thing. I am sure you will need it and then some.

Well, darling, the reason "Daddy" didn't run was that he had to be dignified. He had a doctor with him. How did you know I stood up?

Darling, I certainly did walk when the colonel called me. Because it was the tone used by him that caused me not to come on the double. I shall do the same thing again too, should the opportunity present itself. I swear, Jackie, that it was true.

The reason I explained it that way was so that you would not kiss me too much. You see, I knew you would—and I wanted to be selfish and do all the hugging and kissing myself. It was something swell for me to do. I wanted to see you and everything. I would have done anything to see you.

When next I come home, dear, I would like to read that article about writers.

Dear, now to your trip. I have rechecked my schedule and found this so that you won't have to have a layover in Richmond so very long. This is what you do. It will call for your leaving several hours earlier. Here's the dope. Get a 7:13 a.m. train from Baltimore, and then get the 8:00 a.m. from Washington for Richmond. Your ticket will no doubt read from Washington to Richmond via R.F. & P. Should you not make this one because of the crowd or the like, try the 9:50 a.m. for Richmond. These trains put you in Richmond so that you will be sure to catch the 2:00 p.m. for Newport News. I am sure these trains will be late leaving Washington and late getting into Richmond. It is most likely to be an hour or so late. Either will put you on time for the 2:00 p.m. train. You will, by catching this train, arrive at 3:32 p.m. or thereabouts. I will meet you as my plans are now. In case I should not, go to the inn in a cab—there are plenty of them at the station. Now, about Richmond. Should your train not go to Main Street Station in Richmond, it will go to Broad Street. That being the case, you will have to change, by going from Broad to Main Street Station. You get a colored cab—or white—by following the colored exit signs. Main Street Station has a waiting room where colored cabs can be gotten. He will put you out at Broad Street Station's taxi ramp. Walk through the door down the aisle to the ticket office and turn right. There's the colored waiting room. Everyone goes together to get to the train. Red Cap, Porters, etc. always can tell you what track the train is being loaded on. For the most part, you will find colored coaches next to the engine. Way up front, so to speak. This is particularly true in Washington.

The train conductor will tell you too whether you have to change stations in Richmond upon your asking him.

The train leaving for Richmond from Washington loads on any of the tracks between 22 and 28. Specifically 23 to 26. By checking them fifteen minutes or so, if possible ahead of time, you can maybe get near the front of the line so you can get a head start for a seat. You will have only colored to compete with.

Try to sit near the center of the car—then you will be away from the draft of either door. Sit on the aisle seat. Some windows on some coaches have a draft. Let someone else, if need be, sit next to the window.

Wear too your sport coat—it will be just as warm, I imagine, and far more practical from the point of weight and the ability to take your sport coat. And your coat collar won't get in the way. It won't pick up as much dirt and dust either. Were I you, my purse would be smaller and less likely to get in the way.

Oh yes, if your coach is crowded before you get on it, they may have a women's lounge—in preference to standing, you can sit in it.

Buy a round-trip ticket from Baltimore to Newport News.

Darling, I know I have steamrolled you, but I think this will really help you. Bring your small new bag.

There may be some changes in this, but from what I have written, you may be guided enough to form an opinion all your own on what to do next should something arise. I know you will come out OK.

Should you arrive and I not be there, you can contact me or get information by calling Norfolk 4-5471 extension 167. This too can be put on a telegram. It would help in getting the message to me sooner. I could act accordingly.

What I put in your noon letter about clothing, do that if you can. It may help you.

I know you are wondering why I don't want you so sharp and everything. It's just because I want you to enjoy your trip as much as possible. And above all, we want to be together. Right, darling?

I have paid for our room and everything. Darling, I am hoping I left no stone unturned. Above all, rest as much as you can so that you can't think of catching cold or the like.

I am going to send this special. I hope it gets to you in time.

Darling, I am going to close now. Just for safety's sake, you may not get the letter from this morning. Here's the address of where we shall stay.

Cosmos Inn. 618 Jefferson Avenue, near Twenty-Fifth Street. Phone 2-9486. Newport News, Virginia.

Darling, I shall close now for sure.
With all of me, I am forever yours.

Your husband,
Phil

P.S. Darling, I am mad about you, honest.

February 22, 1943
Monday night

My beloved darling,

I am starting your letter, sweets, where it's going to end. I am going to let this letter tell you.

I got over to the base OK. I got a cab just as soon as I left the building. Anyhow, it made the ferry, which left at 5:45. I got in camp at ten minutes of 7:00, and was eating my breakfast at 7:15.

I came back to my barracks at about 8:30 and tried to call you and could not get a line off the base. I wanted so much to call you, but I just couldn't make it.

Sweetheart, I worked most of the day. Kept myself busy all the morning; this evening, I went to class. Tomorrow, I will take my platoon to the boats to work. I will be there all day.

At 5:25 p.m., I got your telegraph message over the phone saying that you had a pleasant trip home. See, I am glad that you did, darling. Did we leave anything behind? Darling, I kept worrying about you. Why, I can't exactly say, but really I was quite relieved.

Sweetheart, may I say every moment I spent with you this past weekend was a glorious one. Honestly, my beloved, I can't begin to say how much I love you for doing what you did. Really you are a darling wife. I can't begin to kiss you to make up for all that is owed you for your kindness.

You talk about having a swell husband. I have a gem for wife, and you are it. Darling, every time I think of it, I thank God for me being your husband and for having such a grand wife. I shall do that forever, my beloved. I swear it, Jackie, my darling. I love you "a whole lot."

Thanks a million, darling, for sending the telegram. It was more than sweet of you. I can't begin to tell you how much it meant to me. Thanks again, many times.

I got your Wednesday letter today. It made me feel grand as usual. Even though it was late, it was just like getting a letter in regular sequence. Honest, it was really all right.

Oh yes, Hurst has started to get "crabby" already. I told him that would happen anyway—just as soon as he married and his wife got away from him. At times, I suppose, I even get the same way. How about you?

It is quite pleasant here. A real spring day. I did not have to wear my field jacket all day. The weather and I are getting along quite well. I just hope we continue to do so.

All of me, Jackie, wants to be where you are. May I be—I pray soon. That's something, isn't it? It's been less than twenty-four hours since I saw you, and already my heart, soul, mind, and body want so very much to have you right here beside me. Darling, all that there is of me, I pledge to you forever—with every ounce of strength that this body of mine possesses.

Darling, I have just about run out of things to talk about, so I will have to close.

Dearly beloved, as for my love, you need not doubt. I am forever yours—and forever—

—yours, my beloved darling,
Your husband,
Phil

P.S. I bet you can't guess who is in love with you more than you can ever realize. It's I, sweet, your husband. And I am mad about you positively.

Inscribed on the back: This was taken on the same day the battalion photo was taken. I had just come from the docks. These are my work clothes. I'm bowed legged, am I not or do you actually know by experience?

Inscribed on the back:
In this I am sort of large: Am I really that heavy? Why I am a giant? Usually in fact always I carry my head higher, too. In all I hope you like this. That's my platoon. This was taken last January when we went for the parade. That's Harry behind my platoon.

Thursday night
February 25, 1943

Darling Jackie,

When it rains, sometimes it pours, doesn't it? Today I got three letters. Two in the morning, one this evening.

I am going to answer them all tonight and even tell you about myself.

Darling, may I say, first and foremost, I do think a great deal of you. More than that, I am crazy about you, Jackie darling.

Doesn't this pen write a little too thin? Does it make it hard for you to read this writing? If it does, let me know and I will make the proper changes.

Well, here I go, my love. Before I say a word, I don't really know how to say how much getting your letters mean, darling. Honest, darling. For all that I can say, sweetheart, there is no way I could really tell you how much I appreciate your having your mail pile up on me in the manner in which it did. Just wait until I take you in my arms. Then you will know and then some. Honest, you just wait.

Naturally, I am glad you got home so safely. Really I am quite relieved.

I certainly hope you will like your new minister. With the drive most West Indians have your church, now should go a long ways. Right?

Do you get this perfume on this page? Hurst put it there. It's called Follow Me. How do you like it? His wife gave it to him while he was on leave. He is supposed to put it on himself each night and think of her.

That's awful, dear, their keeping awake so late particularly after you had planned to go to bed so early. If it isn't Mrs. Gladden[3], it is someone else keeping you awake so late. Well maybe soon you will be able to strike the happy medium. That will be OK, won't it?

---

[3] Mrs. Gladden is the person Jack rented a room from.

You must have laughed your head off when Lois[4] said she wanted an apartment by herself. If she only knew the trials and tribulations you went through to get a room, she would settle for a great deal less.

Emily is lucky, but she should not be so happy. She should take a cue from that. If Uncle Sam[5] doesn't want him, she must not be getting so much.

I did find out about my rationing book, but I will have to wait until March 15 to reap it.

I liked that article about teachers. You and "me" both say "amen." Darling, the thing to be proud of is that you are trying to live that verse with all your strength. That makes it important.

When I read the paragraph wherein p_____ was mentioned, I had to laugh. Maybe I was tired, but that didn't stop me from being disappointed. I shall rest from now until then (when I see you). That will be next weekend as my plans are.

I have been getting in bed at around eleven o'clock each night and getting up at about seven or seven thirty in the morning. Plenty of sleep.

You did an excellent job of reducing your suit's cost. You did a very good job. The way I see it, you should get your check the early part of the month along with what I should send you. I won't mention any amount because if I do—you know me, I just won't do it.

Nancy's plans went a little off, didn't they? Was she to have the baby? She can't teach now, can she? That's an unusual situation, her being that way. Why does her mother have to brag so much? Someone is going to insult her one day about her children.

Darling, when next I come home, I shall get the sheets and bring them down. That will save you the trouble of sending them down to me.

It's swell you gave Mrs. Gladden the wine. It's really one of those ways you show her that you really appreciate her doing what she does.

Oh baby, as soon as I saw you, my throat got perfect and has been the same since. Darling, I do forgive you.

---

4   Lois and Emily are unknown but sounds like they are also roomers at Mrs. Gladden's.

5   Uncle Sam is a reference to the United States Government

Hurst's wife got home OK at 7 a.m. She was indeed lucky.

We should have given them something. But I was so busy trying to make love to you that I forgot about them. That's the honest truth, my darling. We really did though. I lent him that change.

Phil's[6] lucky to get his two weeks. I bet he is blowing his top.

Now, darling, your husband. He did as follows: get down to the office at 7:50 a.m. and do paperwork on his platoon until noon. That is, sold insurance, sign-up men on government family allowances and their other problems until now, plus get them together for a physical checkup.

This afternoon, I went to the hospital in town so I could get an X-ray and urinalysis—for an increase in my insurance. That's really a job. I may get it through next month. I got back at 2:30 p.m. and made plans for my job tomorrow. Hurst and I have been made inventory officers for our post exchange. We have to count everything in the PX. I will tell you tomorrow just how it is. I am sure I shall cuss the job out. It's only for tomorrow however.

Saturday and Sunday, I am company duty officer and battalion duty officer. That's why I won't be home this weekend. But with my plans as they are, I shall be home the following weekend.

I'm OK, darling, in every respect. The weather here is still pleasant, but not the same warmth.

Darling, I am going to try to close your letter now. Lack of material. OK.

With all my heart, darling, I love you so very much. It is a love that is best spoken of in your poems—that have been in your letters for the last three days. They have been very, very good.

> Yours I am forever,
> Your husband, darling,
> Phil

P.S. Darling, with me, you are mine for all time. I love you, my beloved.

---

6   This is Jack's oldest brother.

Hurst in the middle and Phil on the right. Soldier unknown on left.

Saturday, 9:30 p.m.
February 27, 1943

My beloved darling,

I wonder if you feel as I do now. My first time not seeing you over the weekend since I left OCS[7].

Really, Jackie, I am lonesome and a little dejected. As the night wears on, I am filling up more and more—you know what I mean. There is no doubt about it, Jackie darling. I do miss you so very much—much more, sweets, than you can really think of. Honest.

It's meant so much to be with you all these weekends, that even if I have schemed so much—that this week I can't—I still want so very much to hold you in my arms and kiss and hug, and yes, caress you too. Just our arms about each other means a great deal, sweetheart. You can't begin to realize how much either. Oh well, we have one comforting thought. Next week, with God's will, we shall be together. It shall mean so much for us to be together. Jackie, my darling, with all the strength my lady possesses, I do love you. There is no one on this earth who can or shall ever be able to take your place. You are, in no uncertain terms, my one true love, my dearest wife.

I know you are wondering whether I have been drinking or the like, but to the contrary, I haven't even had a soda. So you see, I am really saying all this from a clear head.

Yesterday, Friday, Hurst and I spent most of the morning inventorying the post exchange. We finished around 11:30 a.m. Now all we have to wait for are extensions and auditing to be done by another office and then sign the report. Then we will be through with that. The afternoon was spent doing various things. At five thirty, we were told that we had to go to Newport News to work all night. Pollard and I went. I will have to wait until I get home to tell you about it. It was messy. It rained, snowed, sleeted, and God knows what else. And it got down

---

7   Officer Candidate School abbreviation

to zero weather. After a general mess up this morning, we got back at about eight thirty. I got in bed around 9:30 and slept until 4:30 p.m. I arose, ate supper, and checked on things around the company and the battalion. Came back to the barracks and talked with first one fellow and then another until they all left. All are gone now except myself and the officer's orderly. They have all gone to a big party in town. It's supposed to really come on. I imagine it shall. There will be many a lie told about it tomorrow. All of them will be in because tomorrow the men are to be paid.

Somehow, I did not get a letter today or yesterday. No doubt I shall have a rainstorm of mail Monday. Which will be OK with me.

My reason, dearest, for not writing last was my having to work. I hope I can get this letter off tomorrow so you can get it maybe Monday evening.

Sweetheart, the day was quite chilly. Was it that way in Baltimore?

That reminds me, darling, don't have Cill[8] stay with you next Friday night. I am going to try to get away Friday night, and if that be so, I will be home early Saturday morning. I am praying, darling, that it will go off just right.

Darling, I am OK as I can be. I don't have a cold, or ache, or pain as of this moment. I can't promise you about tomorrow morning though.

Dear, should you get your check, let me know. I am expecting you to get ahead of the time that you did when I started my last allotment. This form has been in a long time. At any rate, I shall send you your money as soon as I get my check and get it cashed.

Darling, I can't think of much else to write, so I will start to close, OK?

Darling, for a kiss or hug, what I wouldn't do to receive either. You wouldn't want me to talk about it, but I shall try to wait.

---

[8]   This is Jack's sister.

Yours I, and my darling wife,
Your husband,
Phil

P.S. Darling, I love you much more than you have the least idea of. Therefore, I can safely say I'm terribly and madly in love with you, Jackie sweetheart.

Tuesday, 7:30 a.m.
March 2, 1943

Darling,

You must forgive me for not writing last night, but I certainly shall make up for it tonight.

I went to a party last night that Grosby was giving for Hurst, and when I got back at about one o'clock, the beer and bourbon had me. I couldn't write. I was too low. But I was a gentleman, darling.

Sweetheart, I am going to send this letter. I have your money order in this letter—$75.00.

Your Thursday letter came yesterday. Did you make me feel swell? I can't begin to tell you how much.

Sweetheart, I do love you so very, very much. More really than you have the least idea of. Honest.

I am going to close now, Jackie sweets. Until later in the day, OK?

Yours I am forever, dearest,
Your husband,
Phil

P.S. Jack, my love, I shall love you forever, and forever, yours. I am your husband, "that guy," Phil.

Inscribed on the back:
That's Grosby in the bed. I sleep over him. On Sunday our room is a mess.
That's why it looks so bad. Hurst sleeps in the bed where you see the books.
The steps lead to the gym. It's a short cut. A white fellow took the picture. It
came out rather well.

Tuesday, 2:10 p.m.
March 2, 1943

My beloved darling,

Here I am really starting your letter. The one I wrote this morning was merely to send you that money. Here's the one that's going to bill your morale. Or did the one I wrote this morning help some too?

Honest, I am sorry that I didn't write you last night, but you know how it is. That reminds me too—I didn't write you Sunday either. So your husband has a mess of explaining to do, hasn't he?

Darling, I am writing your letter in the office. Well, you know Johnson and Pollard are "B.S. ing?" I write a word and then stop and have to start again. Do you mind, sweetheart?

I am awfully sorry that you dropped your pen. If you can't get one, let me know, and I will bring you one from here.

Dear, I know you are glad that the rationing is over. How on earth could people do a thing like keeping the book so very dirty and filthy? But they will do things like that.

Tell Country Aunt Georgia[9] that as soon as I can, I shall drop her a line, but you know the story to tell her, don't you? That's too bad about Miss Gary. She seems to be such a swell kid.

Darling, I didn't mind your writing as you did. Really, I liked the change too.

Bertha is sort of lucky to get back to work again, isn't she?

Darling, every time I think of something to say, someone asks me a question. Then I am lost for a few moments. Just try to think of what you want after they have asked you a question and you are lost. Do you ever have that happen to you?

I got a letter from Hudson yesterday. He's still in the country. And now they have no chance, so he says of going overseas. Soney is now at Camp Lee Quartermaster Officer Candidate School.

---

9   Country Aunt Georgia is one of Jack's great aunts.

He says they are busting up the company as far as possible and starting some new companies in Newark, New Jersey. He expects to get a pass in several days, so he's going to drop in here and see me. I certainly will be glad to see him. Everything he says is very much the same. He is still running the company with Heard playing the usual part.

Now, dear, down to your husband. Saturday night after he finished your letter, he went to sleep. Got up Sunday morning and went to ten o'clock mass on the post. Came back, went up to the company area and inspected, as well as the battalion. I helped the company commander pay off, and somehow we managed to finish up with twenty-one cents over. At least we didn't go in the hole. Then I went around and broke up all crap games by taking the money. I gave it back yesterday evening. I drank enough beer to "BS" with the boys Sunday night until late. Got up early Monday, 6:00 a.m., and started writing up money orders. Got that finished and took the $1500 to town with me and the mail orderly. Three thousand dollars in orders. While down there, he and I walked all over downtown with a .45 on my hip. No one fainted, but they stared like the devil. It really took me most of the day to get that done. I got my check cashed while I was down there too. Last night, when I came in from supper, Grosby called up and asked us to come in for an impromptu party for Hurst. I did. Enjoyed myself most much. Beer and bourbon were mixed, so you know what happened. Really, I just did make it to bed.

Mrs. Hurst is down here for a week. She came in Sunday morning and is going back this Sunday morning. He is rather lucky.

Pollard and I went and came together. Today I have done quite a lot of paperwork. First one thing and then another.

You told me that Hurst would not be able to repay me this month, but true enough, he asked me last night, in between a drink, about postponing the date of payment. Baby, you really are a wizard. You see you had that all figured out.

Did I tell you that I got your Thursday letter yesterday? That's the one from which I am writing now.

I hope I get a letter today from you. Honest.

You are going to be angry for what I am going to do. Near the end of this letter, I am going to tell you something which will I know make you happy.

I just came back from checking the afternoon mail. No letter for me or any of the other officers. That's tough.

Well, what I wanted to tell you later I've got to do it now. Here goes—I have a five-day leave starting Monday, March 8, to Friday, March 12, 1943.

Pray, darling, that everything will move along smoothly. So that I will be able to take care of my leave.

If I can, I will be home Saturday morning about four o'clock. That's providing I have luck. At any rate, I shall certainly be home this weekend. Of course, sweets, I shall be home as soon as I possibly can. Tomorrow's letter shall have further information. That was dirty to do, wasn't that? Wait until the end of your letter to tell you a thing like that. It's really the truth though. I shall tell you all the details when I shall have taken you in my arms and whispered sweet nothings in your ear.

Darling, I can't think of much else to write, so I am going to try to close.

Jackie, my sweetheart darling, as long as there is a heaven above, I shall love you and then a long time afterward.

Sweetheart, with all my heart and soul, I am mad about you.

Yours with all my heart and love,
Your husband,
Phil

P.S. Darling, I am more than madly in love with you. I am crazy about you. I swear it.

Inscribed on the back: This was taken outside my Sergeant's Quarters. Most of my Sergeants are men old enough to be my father but I get along with them alrite. They are playing Whist in the photo.

Inscribed on the back: That little hat is a part of our winter regalia. When this was taken I was on my way to lunch, Sunday.

Wednesday, 3:15 p.m.
March 3, 1943

My beloved darling,

Here I go again. This letter won't be long, I can bet you on that. Want to bet?

I am taking a break on my paperwork, plus the fact that I am going out tonight to a banquet and cocktail party given by the Chesterfield Club of Norfolk for all of us. With all the things I will have to do in such a short space of time, I wouldn't have the time to do for you (write) what I would want.

Darling, I no doubt shall enjoy myself to the nth degree. It will be probably the first and last time that all of us officers shall be together. So we are expecting a lot of this affair. Even the duty officer won't have to stay on the post; he can go. I hope we can take a photo of us, then I will have some more for our scrapbook.

Dearest, I got your very lovely Monday letter this morning. I wonder what happened to Friday's and Saturday's and Sunday's.

We had equally as busy days Monday, didn't we? I am glad you got my letters. That was rather good for them though. The mail situation is rather poor coming in here. It is a good thing they keep me busy. I would go down there and give them hell on being so lax.

Hurst does put the perfume on at night because his wife told him to do it. Some fellow, isn't he? Or is it she?

Dearest, at this moment it is snowing and sleeting. In general, it is trying to be frosty so far as the weather is concerned. I am doing all right though, sweets. As of this moment, I am right in there.

Sweetheart, Saturday really can't come too soon. We shall be together, and then, darling, we shall really come on. That's providing they don't find something extra for me to do. Which will happen on the drop of one's hat.

Jackie, I am terribly glad you are feeling so well. Naturally, we both shall be feeling very, very, very fine when we get together for those five days. Shall we not, darling? I am planning to do that, baby, really come on—from way back.

Dearest, I am going to go over and check on the afternoon mail. Maybe I shall have some luck.

Darling, I liked that verse you put at the end of your letter. It was the thing.

I went over and got, would you believe it, Tuesday's or yesterday's letter. How can mail be that way?

I shall answer your letter tomorrow though rather than today. OK, sweets?

Dearest, I am going to close now—not because I want to, but because of the circumstances. I bet you are saying in your mind, "Phil must be half-high the way he is writing this letter." Yeh, I am crazy about you, Jackie. Honestly, not kidding.

Darling, with all of me, I am yours.

> Yours I am forever, Jackie
> Your husband,
> Phil

P.S. Sweetheart, not only am I mad about you, but I am also crazy and in love with you.

March 9, 1943
Friday, 8:30 p.m.

My darling dearest,

Here I go again, dearest, on a letter which I hope sincerely will be just what you have been waiting for.

Darling, I have definitely started to miss you—very much. Honest. You will be able to detect it throughout my letter as it goes on.

My love, I had an avalanche of mail. I got your Wednesday and Thursday letter plus James's[10] letter. It was swell getting them, darling.

Here yesterday it rained only in showers. You all got the worse end of the deal.

It was good that you found class more interesting.

I do feel so very sorry for Alice; it would be grand if she and Clifton could get along together. She and he could really get along if they would only do so.

They seem to be closing up quite a number of places all over the place because of their being a menace to health. They have quite a number of spots here in Norfolk and Newport News on that list.

Monday night, I did drink quite a bit of beer. I should have told you. I did get a little high just as I said I would.

Congratulations on your having done what you did. Of course, I knew your lessons would be OK anyway.

I really must have put you through the mill last week. Why, you have been terribly sleepy all week.

I am glad you have found a cure for your feet, and that you have found out why your feet are as they are. Isn't that liniment some strong? Darling, you will go until you get your feet in perfect shape, please. Then I can step on your feet when I get ready.

Your telling your kids about giving the money to Red Cross should they mess up reminds me of my having told my men if they don't respect

---

[10]   James is Phil's oldest brother.

my mess hall properly, I will close it up and eat the food myself. They laughed at me because they knew I was joking.

Today, I did quite a bit of paperwork in the battalion for the men in the platoon. I got two shots—which, of all I have taken, did not affect me as these have done. My left arm is hardly raisable. Thank God they were and are the last for quite some time.

The sun has shone quite brightly today, and I have worked around in my shirt sleeves. My cold is gone too. I hope.

James's letter had the usual things in it. I shall answer it Sunday. In fact I shall answer all my correspondence then. I hope.

Sweetheart, I am going to close your letter now, for want of material.

Yours I am forever, my love,
Your husband,
Phil

P.S. Darling, I swear I am mad about you. A whole lot.

Phil with his brother James

Thursday, 11:45 p.m.
March 18, 1943

My darling,

After having done a number of things, now I am going to pen you my daily missive of love.

I got your Tuesday night letter today. You found your perfume, didn't you? I like it, despite it's being a change from that which you have been using.

Dearest, I am glad your foot is improving, and above all that you are feeling quite well. Keep it up, darling.

Today, I got a letter from Annie Laurie[11]. It was the same stuff as usual. Mr. Alexander is up. She is going to Gary, Indiana, to visit her sister this summer—so she says and hopes. Otherwise, everything is going along quite well.

Sweets, you certainly shall have to get to work on your correspondence. So shall I. I have some three or four letters to write myself. That was awfully nice of you to think to send my aunt the photos, Jackie. Pop[12] is really coming on, isn't he? I wonder what next.

The warmth of these days do get me a little drowsy, but somehow, I manage to stay awake. Today that was particularly true.

My arms are OK. I shall get some more shots tomorrow and next week, and then I suppose I am through. I hope. "And my hair not fuzz on my chest is OK." – Mrs. Kane!!!! ____!!!??!!

Today, I moved about quite a bit. First I had my platoon on the ships, and then in the meantime, I helped work the requisition. And finally this evening I worked on the ships. After supper, I went to school, came back, BS'ed, and bathed. And here I am almost ready to close your letter.

---

[11]   Annie Laurie was the daughter of the family that Jack stayed with when visiting Phil in Mississippi.

[12]   This is a reference to Jack's father.

I am OK in every respect. Darling, with all my heart and soul, may I say: as ever, I am yours forever.

You're my darling,
Your husband,
Phil

P.S. I love you, dear. Honest!

Annie Laurie

Sunday, 12:30 p.m.
March 21, 1943

My darling,

I am starting your letter after having postponed writing it since early this afternoon. Since I returned from the movies around 8:30 p.m., I have been sitting around BS-ing and drinking beer. Can you imagine my doing that?

Gee, it's been raining and hailing something awful here all day long. I don't know what to think of this first day of spring. How's the weather in Baltimore today?

My love, I got your Friday letter today. As usual, sweet, it made me feel quite great to get it. Honest, my darling.

Darling, I am so glad you are feeling so very well. Keep up the good work, my love, and should I get a chance to come home next weekend, I shall most assuredly have a special kiss and hug for you. Honest, Jack, no kidding. Dearest, remember the hug and kiss that I gave you last Sunday for this Sunday? I just thought of it. I am glad I gave it to you. Really, it meant a lot to me.

Hudson, dear, is doing OK. He is going on maneuvers in Tennessee for the next two months. Therefore all passes and furloughs have been cancelled. I hope I am still in the vicinity when he does come here in July as he plans to.

Hurst is in New York over the weekend. He left Friday night and called today to say he would be in late tomorrow morning. His probable reason for not going out is that he is broke. Hence he stays home.

Thanks a million, darling, for wanting to help me continue do a good job. I love you most for that, darling. I swear it, my love.

Why don't you scribble a few lines about that guy (your husband)? You can't tell what might happen.

Last night I went to the movies and saw *Margin for Error* with Joan Bennett and Milton Berle. It was good. Likewise, tonight's *Three Hearts for Julia* with Ann Sothern and Melvyn Douglas. I enjoyed both. They were comedies of a fashion with a little seriousness in each of them.

There is still not enough in any of the pictures I have seen to cause me to write a lot about them.

I went to church this morning as per usual and came back and wrote all my letters—James, Hudson, and Annie Laurie. Send me Britt's[13] address so I can write him a bread-and-butter letter[14] for that evening of fun, so to speak.

Sweetheart, my cold is OK now. I am going to do everything to keep it that way.

My love, do you mind if I try to close our letter now? I have just about run out of stuff to talk about. I shall have more to say tomorrow, however.

Yours I am forever, my beloved,

Your husband,

Phil

P.S. My sweet, with all of me, I am deeply in love with you—"a whole lot."

---

[13]   Britt was a high school friend.

[14]   This is a thank you note

March 23, 1943
Tuesday, 9:31 p.m.

My sweetheart,

I have just returned from school—a class, to be specific. It was from 7:30 to about 9:15. Some old stuff that I have been messing around with for the last few days, weeks. It was fairly interesting.

Darling, I got your Sunday letter today, plus your last-night letter (Monday's). Both were killer dillers, particularly Monday's. I have a special spanking for you on that account. You really in every sense of the word came on. I am going to try not to answer your letter (Monday's) tonight, but answer it tomorrow night because I have a hunch that I won't get any mail tomorrow. I hope though that I will be able to drop home this weekend. Should I be able to, I would be right in there if I could see you in your new outfit. You wouldn't mind wearing it for me, would you? However, save aside about $5.00 for me. I shall arrive quite broke per usual. OK?

My love, really I am awfully sorry that I disappointed you over the weekend. Would that I could have come home, you can bet your bottom dollar that I would have been right in your arms.

Pollard was telling me about this picture *Gentleman Jim*. I am really going to try and see it when it comes this way. You know how I like a good fighting picture.

That was awful about the minister having to wait all that time. The things that do happen these days aggravate one to no end. I know how he must have felt.

No doubt Spike[15] is on his way to an overseas post. I don't think—in fact, I am sure—that he is where such a card as that is sent.

Bea[16] did really come on, didn't she? She's saying in so many words that Phil's my man, and no other chick is going to take over.

---

[15] Spike is Phil's sister, Mary's boyfriend.

[16] Bea is Phil's, Jack's brother, girlfriend who is referred to later in the sentence.

Darling, with the constant urging that you give me from time to time, why, I will do more than just get recommendations. I will get promotions too, I hope.

Baby, I am going to try not to work too hard this week, but I am willing to bet you anything that I will be pushed to the nth degree the last part of this week.

Tomorrow night, I have to go to a meeting to get the setup. On the way, they are going to inventory the post exchange. Hurst and I are to do that job again. This time it is much worse. On top of inventorying, we have to make extensions—which are a definite job. I will tell what it is when I get home. I am willing to wager that something else quite aggravating will come up before, so I will have to put out some extra energy.

Today, I took my platoon down for some more rigging and stowing of dummy cargo. I and they learned quite a lot for a change.

Darling, can you guess what I had for supper? Marconi and beets and nothing else. I ate out of the post exchange. Now off that stuff for me. The men have been getting very good chow for eighteen or twenty days, so tonight, every one of them, after they got their plates filled, looked at me as a hungry child looks at its parents. I told them, "Don't look at me." That's just a meal they will have to chalk up against Uncle Sam. They laughed. It was a funny thing though.

Today has been a cool one. I had on quite a number of clothes, which is a usual thing when it gets cool. The sun shone quite brightly.

Darling, I have run out of things for this letter. Tomorrow night more, right?

With all of me, darling, I am yours forever and a day.

Yours, my honey dumpling,
Your husband,
Phil

P.S. I love you tremendously, dear. Honest.

Jack's brother, Philip Jones

March 24, 1943
Wednesday, 9:15 A.M.

My darling,

I know it seems strange that I would be writing you at this time of the morning. But nothing has come down for me to do yet, so I could think of nothing better than to write you. I know I should be reading some book about stevedoring or some other military matter, but after all, with my mind dug into that stuff almost all the time, why, you wouldn't mind my stopping to pen you a few words, would you, darling?

This morning thus far is pleasantly chilly, if you get what I mean. So far as I am concerned, it could stay that way. Knowing this weather to be so changeable, this afternoon might hold for me a blizzard.

Every time I read your Monday letter, I am thoroughly of the belief that you were in a quite mischievous mood. The letter that you wrote brought all that out quite emphatically. I am not kidding when I say— as I read it over and over again—I am really buoyed up, so to speak, by the contents of it. Honest, old lady, it was really a swell letter. Just the kind your husband needs so very much.

Dear, I can't wait hardly to see how you look in your suit Sunday. I bet you are as sharp as tack. And I mean sharp!

Mildred J. Seaborne and Gwendolyn Lynch in a way will have quite a time, won't they? I wonder how Mildred will come out of it. And Ella [17] too. What does Ms. Nichols think of her marrying a fellow who is tall and dark?

In your letter writing, you covered as much growth as myself. I wrote several letters to various people too, so now we are up on our mail.

Your burning your arm is no doubt responsible for your saying a certain little word, but you blamed it on the way you were writing your letter. Though, I will admit, I did say what you said, plus a number of

---

[17]   These women are all former high school classmates.

other things. But no kidding, it was cute your saying that. And "variety is the spice of life."

Baby, I am through with needles for a while. I hope, at least, that Friday I took the last one.

As to Annie Laurie. Mrs. Kane, I am of the opinion that that is a matter which we'll have to discuss verbally. Right? My fuzz is growing too, but I assure you that from now on, because you call my hair fuzz, I will be forced to stop you from running your hands through it.

That, darling, must have been quite disappointing, to have thought I called you and didn't. Honest, sweets, I would have done everything to have been there. But I will do all I can to be there this weekend.

Dearest, of course, I shall stay free of colds. And I won't imbibe too much.

Your poem at the end of your letter really came on—as they always do. No kidding.

Well, sweets, I am going to close now—not because I want to in any way, but because the lack of material says so.

Jack, my darling, with all my heart and soul, I am forever yours.

Yours, my beloved sweetheart,
Your husband,
Phil

P.S. I love you terribly much, dear. Do you mind?

Sunday, 7:50 p.m.
April 11, 1943

My beloved darling,

Please forgive me, dearest, if this isn't as good a letter as you have formerly gotten. Sweetheart, though you have been gone only about twelve hours, I am all messed up. I am thinking of you, and already, sweetheart, I wish I could hold you in my arms and squeeze you so tightly.

Beloved, I got your telegram around 5:30 or 6:00 p.m. Gosh, darling, I am glad everything is really OK. Particularly that you got away OK. I checked your train time on leaving and found that you were to leave twenty minutes ahead of the time that I had told you that you were supposed to leave. Will you forgive me, dearest? No doubt, you got home before you had really expected to.

I made it to the base on the streetcar and arrived around 7:40. I was in the office at 8:00 a.m. We had the inspection and so forth. It was over at 10:15. The colonel said there was a definite improvement in the men. Naturally, I agree with him.

I came up (barracks) and called Mrs. Sutton. She told me of how many places she called to get a taxi. She was very surprised at your leaving the money. She praised you to the skies. Naturally, all I could say was that she was right in doing that because you are just everything. I went to the 11:15 mass and came back for lunch, and lo and behold, the colonel and the major were back for lunch again. So I had quite a crowd. An important one too. The rest of the afternoon, I spent reading and sleeping and hoping that everything was going along well with you. Tonight, I have saved a little of everything—got men from town who had gotten over the fence without a pass, settled arguments and fights. As for myself, I am OK. I did not get hurt or anything.

There is no need saying how much your being with me this past week has boosted my morale. Though we had our ups and downs per usual, nevertheless we did have so much fun just being with each other. Sweetheart, I shall not forget last night. It was all ours and a one of love too. Jackie, my darling, honest, with all of me, you are mine. And forever I shall be yours. For one who is as sweet as you are, I have a million bear hugs and as many kisses as you can think of. And then some.

I am going to make reveille with the men tomorrow morning. I have got to check up on the men. I think they are beginning to ease up too much.

I shall get those pamphlets from the USO for you, and I shall return Mrs. Sutton's key. I forgot to leave it this morning in the hurry.

My darling, I am going to start to close now—not because I want to, but because I can't do any better.

Yours with all my heart and soul, I shall be forever.

Your husband,
Phil

P.S. Darling, I love you tremendously and a whole lot. Honest.
P.S. Darling, if I could let you know in time, could you come down Saturday morning and stay until Sunday night? I mean, could you arrange that? Let me know in your next letter so if it is possible, I could telegram you in time so you could catch the Saturday morning train. If you want more details, ask them too.

Saturday, 2:30 p.m.
April 17, 1943

My beloved darling,

I am writing you so that on Monday you will get a letter from me. I got one from you today; it was Tuesday's, and as usual it made me feel great. Of course, your being so very close to me (Norfolk) puts far more emphasis on our being so very much in love.

Dearest, I am sitting here praying that tomorrow we will be able to be together. They keep talking about our company having to work all day, and then again they say only Sunday night. I hope it's Sunday night they mean.

Darling, you know, as I think of us, we have spent a lot time going through things that other people never experience. But it goes toward making us love each other more. Though it was inconvenient for you to come down here with me Friday night, it was to me something thrilling. It made me feel great kissing you in the dark and going to sleep on your shoulder. It was just like being your baby. I am really that, you know—all yours too!

You are no doubt home now, sleeping or day-dreaming of us. I am thinking of us too. Darling, you know what? I hope that I can stay awake tonight to love you as you want to be. It's such an exhilarating feeling to love you, Jackie, until you tingle all over and just feel waves and waves of passionate ecstasy course through your body. Darling, every time I think of you, I want my heart to skip a beat. Honest, darling, that's just what it wants to do. You see, I am crazy about you. Madly in love with you—far more, Jackie darling, than you shall realize ever. Sweets, I am yours. That I shall be—ever yours.

Jackie, I know you are wondering why I am writing you as I am, but you see, I am a crazy guy. You know that, don't you? But as I said before, I am crazy about you! Yes, you, darling.

Darling, I am going to try to close. With all my heart and soul, Jackie darling, I am yours.

Yours, my darling wife,
Your husband,
Phil

P.S. Darling, I love you—a whole lot. Honest. I swear it.

April 18, 1943
Sunday, 4:39 p.m.

My darling wife,

I have not so very long come over from Newport News. Gee, it's chilly here. Maybe it's because I'm so very close to the water. We worked in a warehouse, which is built over the water. The dampness just crept up and hung on for a while. It came on in a short way. I am a little chilly right now, that's why my handwriting is so very poor right now. I am waiting for supper. It better be good because I am hungry.

Darling, you know I want to write a lot, but somehow, I can't think of a lot to say. But I can say this much: the past week is one which shall indeed be a memorable one. Particularly your coming down here Friday. My leaving you this morning so very early was a miracle. How did you get me to do it? All the thanks goes to you, darling. Sweetheart, my calling you Sunday before you left made my day full and lifted my morale very, very much. I was honestly walking on air for at least two hours. I could not even eat all my lunch. Filled to the brim with love, can you imagine that?

Jackie, my beloved, it may seem crazy of me to say it, but I shall and will be yours for a very, very long time. More than you can ever imagine, darling. I am forever yours.

I am going to close now, Jackie. Lack of material. I shall have oodles to write you tomorrow. I promise, dear.

Yours I am forever, sweetheart,
Your husband,
Phil

P.S. Sweetheart, I love you a whole lot. Honest.

April 19, 1943
Monday, 2:07 p.m.

My darling wife,

I am starting your letter hoping that I won't be called away before I finish it.

Dearest, it's just to start your letter now because the very first thing I want to do is tell you how much I love you. How much I shall continue to love you and so forth. Dearest, I do love you with all my heart and soul. I shall always love you. Forever and a day, yours I shall be—longer than you can ever imagine. Plus all that, my beloved. I have a whole lot of loving for you. Honest.

Naturally, my luck on letters for today is nil, but maybe the next day.

This morning I worked on the ships until it started pouring downstairs. We have stopped working and have been waiting for them to call us back to work. It has cleared up quite a bit now, and we may go back soon. I hope we do, so we won't have to work at least on the ships on Saturday.

Dearest, all the boys are doing OK. Even I am OK.

Darling, I want to write more, but you know how it goes. Daddy is running out of stuff to write about.

Last night, I went to see a movie called *Corregidor*. It "stank." No good. Tonight, I may do several of several things. I may go to see *Cabin in the Sky* or *Hangmen Also Die!* It's according to how sleepy I am. I went to bed about 11:30 p.m. and did not wake until 7:10 a.m. Some sleeping, wasn't it? You see, I should rest up for your coming again, shouldn't I? I shall do my best to be well rested when I see you Thursday night.

Dear, I got your telegraphic message at about 10:30 p.m. Gosh, darling, I feel great inside to know that everything went along swell for you. If you got home at 7:40 p.m., you didn't have to wait for any trains at all. You just got off one and got on the next one. That's luck, darling. Were you able to do much work like reading and fixing up your race book? If you did, you came on. It was far different than your trip coming down here.

Darling, I wrote for more than I thought I could, but you see what happens when you continue to try to write. Maybe if I wrote for another fifteen minutes, I would be OK and write you a ten-page protestation of love.

Sweets, I am going to close now for sure.

Yours I am forever, my beloved.

Your husband,
Phil

P.S. Darling sweetheart, I love you a whole lot. I swear I do.

Monday night
April 26, 1943

My beloved darling,

Here I go on my usual sort of stuff. Darling, I am waiting, so to speak, for your telegram.

I have finished working over at the PX, and now all we have to do is make the extensions. That I intend to make last at least two days.

Darling, I have got to say this before I go another line further. Sweetheart, I do love you so very much, and this past week you made me so very happy. Honest, my beloved, you are so very much mine. Jackie, I will always love you, and a great deal too—far more than you will ever realize. Darling, you may think sometimes that my love may be dropping off just a little, but it isn't, honest; I am just storing it up so I can really come on like a tornado. Memories of ecstasy I will have of us this week. For all your sweetness, loveliness, and unselfishness toward me, I pledge you my eternal love and devotion.

Dear, everyone is back off their leaves. The colonel is no doubt off his high horse. I hope so anyway.

Darling, I must say I was angry when I was made an inventory officer, but there, it's just a job, so I will do my best to make a go of it. I am sure I shall.

Dear, I still can't get a drift on what I will be able to do this weekend. At least I will let you know in time by telegram just what you can expect to do. Rather than come home so weary Saturday, I may take the boat up. I don't know; in preference to going up on the train, I am of the opinion that you may have to come down. But anyway I will let you know in time so that you will know just the preparations.

It is about at 8:10 a.m. Tuesday. I have called Western Union, and they say there is no telegram. I hope everything is OK.

I shall close now hoping that later in the day I shall hear from you.

Yours, my beloved, I shall ever be,
Your husband,
Philip

P.S. Jackie, I love you a whole lot. Honest.

April 27, 1943
Tuesday, 1:30 p.m.

My darling wife,

I have been waiting for a while. We have been working all morning on the inventory. Inasmuch as some infantry officers, one giving the men instructions on rifle marksmanship, we won't have anything to do. Hence we have to spend as much time as we want on this job. Isn't that something, darling? Just as soon as you leave, they stop having so much work for me to do.

I betcha if you came down here they would have something else to do. That would be tiring and nerve-wracking. Well, just to have you down here with me would be OK. They could bring on as much work as they would want.

Sweets, today is pleasant—cool and slightly invigorating. Darling, to hold you in my arms would be indeed like a dream right now. I would squeeze you so tightly. You would say, "Phil, please, you are holding me too tight."

Jackie, I keep thinking about our past weekend. It was indeed grand and glorious. You were so much mine. All mine, darling. You loved me, sweetheart, with every ounce of strength that it was possible for you to muster. Even now I still feel throughout my body waves of exhilarating ecstasy generated by you, slowly ebbing from my being. Jackie, how can I help but try forever to love you? I will, dear, with all my heart and soul.

My love, last night I went to our new movie house to see a picture with Lana Turner and Robert Young in it called *Slightly Dangerous*. It was a comedy. I liked it because she (Lana) did a lot of things that you do—wink your eye, cuddle close to me in a sly way, make me or things you want subtlety, kiss me, send me from way back, and do any number of things I would not expect you to do. You see why I liked it.

Darling, I am going to go back to work now, but before I do, here's a million kisses for you.

Darling, has school been tiring today? I hope it hasn't. Did you have very much trouble with your bags? In general, did you have a hard trip?

With every desire to be with you, dear, I am yours forever.

Yours forever, Jack,
Your husband,
Phil

P.S. Darling, with love, I say I love you a whole lot.

August 18, 1943

Dear Jim,

I got the letter you sent to me through Jackie. Fella, you are really coming on back there in the states. More power to you. I enjoyed the hell out of reading your letters. It really was a treat. As Kanes, we certainly do come on, don't we? You and Big George [18]are raising more hell in the army than ever thought, even if I did make first in four months.

The working is pretty regular. I have my head in a lot of things. I manage somehow to make a good showing for "Happy Feet[19]" Keep in there kid—punching.

Keep up the good work. Jack writes me often. Mom[20] frequently, and Ma[21] several times a week. She really knocks me out with all that keeps stuff in her letters. Sometimes I almost swear I'm getting letters from a hip chick.

Fella, I am wondering if you look sharp in them boots, and breeches. If you do, I reckon I will have to dig a pair too. My only advice to you is not play the chicken too strong. It'll get you down.

Write my old lady often—she likes your jive. Read her this letter, and after you have finished it, I want to see if she will raise hell because I write her something jive. Can't think of much else to say so I will close.

Yours letter.

Happy Feet

It's free. If you get a shot of yourself, knock me one. Frankly, I can't imagine you being or looking like a soldier. Can you stand at attention yet?

---

[18]   This refers to Phil's brother, John.

[19]   This is a Kane family nickname for Phil. His sister Mary gave him this nickname because of the movement of his feet when driving a standard shift car. He regularly drove cars that were unreliable and required coaxing.

[20]   Mom refers to Jack's mother.

[21]   This refers to Phil's mother.

My darling Jackie,

Here are a just a few things. Honestly, I don't like any of them very much. For you, I wanted what I sent you to be definitely unique.

Hence, sweetheart, you can depend on my sending you something at a later date that will really knock you out. When I do find it, my love, you can depend on your having it as soon as possible.

All these are yours, so until I get that which I really want you to have, could these just be a token?

I am yours forever,
Your husband,
Phil

P.S. I am sending Mom and my mother's gift off the same day as yours.

Inscribed on the back: Here you see your hubby playing some fine football. Dig that pose! I have on my fatigues here and field jacket. The other colored fellow is Tom Davis.

December 1, 1943

My darling,

I hope you like this little token of love that is enclosed herein.

I've sent it by airmail, thinking that perhaps you might get it before Christmas.

Lots of love to you, my honey dumpling. I love you always. "a real whole lot."

Honest, Jackie.

Yours forever,
Your husband,
Phil

P.S. I love you a whole lot, OK?

Inscribed on the back: Here is a snap of the court martial scene – held about a month ago. This hall of wood is the largest auditorium in this area. Marian Anderson will sing here on the 25th of January. We have a lot of classes here too. We sit in those seats and take notes – 335 of us. We are really here to get our bars and win this war - when we have to do things like this. But I suppose it is o.k. What do you think about it?

13 January, 1944
Thursday night

My darling wife,

Just a few more lines to add to the rest that I write.

Darling, I'm in a mood tonight. I can't exactly explain it. It's a one that could be dissipated if I could talk to you. I could lay my head on your shoulder and just tell you everything. You could console me, I know. Dearest, so often I need you to talk to and to be with. You are my everything, Jackie. How can I ever be anything but madly in love with you? I know that you are the only one in the world who can make me happy, truly happy.

Today no mail came, except for a Christmas card from my mother but tomorrow may bring a great deal of it. I shall be waiting anyway.

My love I think so much of being in your arms. We would be so happy being together, I know. Keep sweet, sweetheart.

Love and kisses, Jackie

Your husband.
Phil

P.S. Dearest, I love you "a real whole lot."
I always will, too.

15 January 1944
Friday night

My darling sweets

Already this week has passes so quickly that I hardly know what to say. Maybe it is because, I have been a little busy this week. You know how time can fly when you do a lot.

Dearest, I don't know very much to talk about for some reason or other.

Nothing unusual is happening worth writing about, dearest.

Dearest, I am "per usual", just a little bit but that's about you.

The weather here is very pleasant, I am enjoying it very much.

Sweetheart, I love you more than just a little bit, it's a tremendous amount.

I'll close now
Yours forever, sweets

Your husband
Phil

P.S. My love, I love you "a real whole lot."

16 January 1944

Dearest,

This is the note that I said I wrote so that you could send me the Christmas gift.

To whom it may concern:

Request is hereby made for permission for the undersigned wife Mrs. Jacqueline J. Kane to send a package containing articles which the undersigned has requested from time to time.

Dearest, I am sure this will be sufficient. If not, please let me know.

Yours with all of me,
Philip G. Kane
0-1844856
First Lieutenant Corps

16 January 1944
Sunday evening

My sweetheart,

I was more than pleasantly surprised to receive your very sweet January letters. I also received a letter from my mother and one from Britt. As usual they are several days ahead, so I will have to sweat it out waiting for the letters that are in between to come. But it is good to know that they are on their way.

Today has been very pleasant. I have enjoyed it immensely, the fact that it was pleasant and everything. I enjoyed working for it. I have been doing that all day too. I did not get a chance to go to church, but the same old expression there is "Next Sunday." But I did miss going a lot though.

Britt seems to be doing all right. He says he enjoys reading your letters very much. My mother was quite elated over meeting your mother. I am awaiting your letter telling me more of the details. Our mothers sure have been a long time getting to meet each other, haven't they?

Yours forever, darling.

Your husband,
Phil

P.S. I love you "a real whole lot," sweet. Always.

16 January 1944
Sunday evening
Part II

My beloved darling,

Jackie, sweets, I love you. Honest, I do. Gee, honey, I could take you in my arms and just bear hug you so much that you'd have to beg me to let you go.

Needless to say, I know you can use that raise I gave you, but I agree all those deductions are "some stuff," and it could be a great deal worse.

Darling, keep up the good work with your classes. You aren't doing badly at all, are you?

I recall very well how beautiful your display of Christmas cards were last year. I can vividly imagine how much more so they must have been this year. Thanks for the honor. Mine were given.

I bet you were surprised when I told you of my desire to enter the Air Corps. The angle I was working on temporarily fell through. The War Department is holding up applications until later. My application had just been forwarded to the very first base. Oh well, I'll just wait or forget it, whichever is warranted. At any rate, don't worry, and thanks for all that luck you sent me. I am using all of it each day to keep me going.

Your husband,
Phil

P.S. Darling Jackie, I will always be mad about you. I love you "a real whole lot."

16 January 1944
Sunday evening
Part III

My sweet darling,

Thanks a million too, sweet, for sending me the books. I am penning a separate letter so that you can send me those things you had held for Christmas for me. I will get that off tonight, Jackie.

Darling, I will keep my chin up. I am glad the mail is coming though in pretty good fashion and that once in a while, you get a letter that makes you happy. I'll write them as often as I can, dearest. But dear, believe me, my letters can't do half the job that I in person could do. Mrs. Kane, I presume you are aware of that. Should you not be, just wait until I take you in my arms again. I'll prove it all to you.

My darling, I'll write you just as I feel, but I do hope you will be made happier more often than you are made sad. Your letters do the same thing to me. Do you see that we still have a great deal in common? That's why we are so mad about each other. We are just enough alike.

Jack, my angel, keep smiling.

Yours forever,
Your husband,
Phil

P.S. Jackie, honey dumpling, I love you most much. "A real whole lot," to the more definite. Really, I do.

17 January 1944
Monday night

My sweetheart darling,

Dearest, I do hope and pray very much that when you receive this letter, you will be feeling swell in every respect and that you won't be worrying at all about anything.

Sweets, I am feeling per usual—you know how that is, don't you? I don't feel tired yet, but I know I will later tonight. But tomorrow I will sleep it off. Why complain about it?

I did not get any mail today, but I got a lot yesterday, so why again raise a lot of cane?

By the way, you can see that I don't have a lot to say. The rest of your letter will be thus.

Jackie, my sweet, I love you because you are everything to me. You are my true love, my sweetheart, my everything. Really you are, Jack. Honey, I could never tire of letting you know how much I love you. More than that, I will show you, dear, just how much. Just as soon as I can take you in my arms.

Yours with all of me.

Your husband,
Phil

P.S. My cherub of love, I love you "a real whole lot." Forever will I love you too.

18 January 1944
Tuesday night
Part I

My darling love,

With all of me, I am yours with every infinitesimal fiber of my being. I will forever be that way, my darling. I swear it. Can you imagine my writing you this letter with a pair of gloves on? Well, I am doing it, believe it or not. How it is being done is a mystery to me. That's the truth, so help me.

Today, my dearest, I got your January 2 letter. As always, Jackie, I was more than glad to receive it. Honey, it made me feel great by raising my morale a hundred percent. Keep on writing me, honey, and the first thing you know, I will float on air and be right back home and in your arms. But putting all that aside, I did thoroughly enjoy it. I always will too, dearest.

Darling, I am feeling swell, per usual. Honest now, I can't complain about very much. I won't even try.

All in all, though, I do pray that you are in swell shape, dearest. I love you tremendously.

Your husband,
Phil

P.S. Darling, I love you "a real whole lot." Don't you ever forget that because it's true.

18 January 1944
Tuesday night
Part II

My sweet wife,

Well now, really there was quite a houseful that Sunday my mother and yours met. I'm glad Mary[22] did well. Honey, I, like you, am glad that our mothers have met.

Life's artist was not wrong about wha he said concerning "soldiers." It's quite human and realistic. At least, now you know. But why talk about it? The thing we've got to do is get it over with as soon as possible.

Dearest, I shall do as you said, hold up. I can't let you down. I'll give it my all. I can, without giving that which belongs to you. All that must be yours forever.

Darling, I do hope it will be over very soon, just as you said so that this time next year, I can have said that I have been spending my days and nights with you for quite some time.

My love, except for saying the same old things, I am truly mad about you. I always will be too, my love. I swear it, Jacqueline.

Yours I am forever.

Your husband,
Phil

P.S. Darling, I love you tremendously and "a real whole lot." I swear it.

---

[22]   This is one of Phil's sister.

20 January 1944
Thursday night
Part I

My angel love,

Yesterday, I got your December 20 letter. That was quite some time back, wasn't it? But the good part was that I got it, and I am thankful for it.

Oh yes, dearest, before I go further, today I got your January 1 letter. You see, I have a lot of talking I can do to you tonight. I like it too, darling, because in this way, I can get a lot off my mind and chest. Thus, I will feel a great deal better. You won't mind reading it all, will you, Jack?

My mother really did like the Christmas gift you gave her, darling. In her letters, she was quite elated at your giving her the gift. My father was fully satisfied with his too. You see how well you did, and you didn't have a suggestion even from me. A bear hug for you, sweetheart. I owe that, and I will pay it as soon as I take you in my arms. You won't even have to remind me, sweets. That's my promise to you, sweetheart. I love you always.

Your husband,
Phil

P.S. Dearest, I can't ever forget that I will always love you "a real whole lot."

20 January 1944
Thursday night
Part I

My cherub,

"Phil, how do you and why do you think of all those things to say?"
Well, babe, I'll tell you about that later.

I thought you knew Zora Neale Hurston was from Baltimore. I
think she got an honorary doctorate from Morgan the year before I
graduated, or at least the year after.

Honey, you have gotten so far ahead of me on reading and becoming
well read that I won't be able to converse with you. I'll catch up though.

Keep on feeling fine as silk, dear. You know how I feel about your
feeling that way.

Oh yes, you do receive a promotion for making me a first lieutenant
again.

My mother's letters said that everything was sweet. She thinks the
photo was fine. Someone told her the photo looked like that of a girl,
for I look that tender in the face. If I did, from now on, I will take only
full-length photos. I don't want to be called the wrong thing. But she
does think it is one of the best that I have ever had taken.

Darling, I am still an egotist, am I not? That's one of the things I
miss you for so very much—you'd help it so much by saying just the
things.

Yours forever,
Phil

P.S. Darling, keep being mine forever, because I love you "a real whole
lot." Always.

20 January 1944
Thursday night
Part II

Dearest love,

Dear, you know your being sleepy is OK, honey, but when I come home, you must stay awake. Do you think you can?

Oh yes, I got a *Courier*[23] the first of the week and forgot to tell you I get them comparatively regularly. The *Courier* does have some good pinups in it.

It is too bad that the Purviance is that way. It only remains for time to tell whether he will continue to grow worse or better.

The boys are OK. They are putting on so that we can get this thing over.

Darling, you got some practice on how to carry Phil Jr. by carrying Sanford[24]. Do you think you will let our Phil raise all that sand when I carry him? I can well imagine that you don't want to do that again. It is good they are improving a lot, as well as Aunt Georgia[25].

Darling, please don't think about the gifts. When you get the letter that I wrote, you can send them. When I receive them, I will feel swell, and they will mean much to me as if I had gotten them in Christmas.

When do Phil and Bea intend to do that thing, very soon or later?

Yours dear,
Your husband,
Phil

P.S. Darling, I love you "a real whole lot." I won't ever stop either, my love.

---

[23]   This refers to the Pittsburgh Courier, an African-American newspaper published in Pittsburgh, Pennsylvania, from 1907 until October 22, 1966.

[24]   This is Jack's uncle.

[25]   This one of Jack's aunts.

20 January 1944
Thursday night
Part II

Dearest love,

No, the dog hasn't been in my bed since. In fact, he doesn't hang around our camp anymore. I suppose he was just a transient passing through and liked my bed better than the others.

"Sweat out the mail" or anything is an expression over here that means that you will wait for a thing to happen and the anticipation and etc. makes one sweat or perspire.

Darling, you are very brave, courageous, and loyal when you say we must "live on, wait on, hope on, and pray on," despite our not seeing each other. Honest, Jacqueline, if I did not have you to cheer me on, I don't know what I would do. It's only you, and all that you say that makes me want to carry on as you would want me to. I love you for it, dearest.

Per usual, I am OK. A bit tired or beat, but nothing else. I can right now take you in my arms and squeeze you so tight that you would say Phil is still just as strong as ever.

Yours forever,
Your husband,
Phil

P.S. Dearest, I love you "a real whole lot." Honest, honey. Give my love and best regards to everyone.

20 January 1944
Thursday night
Part III

My dearest love,

Sweets, we will have nights that were made for us. You just wait and see.

I was just going to ask you if Gail Carter has written anything about us in the *Afro*[26]. You know, I am glad that you can keep up with us by reading the papers. Not so bad, is it? I told him specifically that it was my brother, and he asked who the athlete was. That just goes to show how much he wanted me to be an athlete.

As soon as I get my next *Courier*, I will let you know the expiration date. I'd like to have now the *Afro* too. Continue your clippings by all means, but you don't have to send those which are in the *Afro*. There are others that you send which I would like for you to continue. You will, won't you?

The fellows are doing pretty well. I didn't know Elaine Curry had that many children, but then again, I have been away from home for better than two and a half years, so that could be the reason.

That's tough they are doing Iris's name that way. Harry is doing a very good job of being an ideal husband over here. Well, such is life.

Yours, dear,
Your husband,
Phil

P.S. Dearest, with all my might, I enjoy loving you through eternity. I love you "a real whole lot." Honest.

---

26   Refers to the Baltimore Afro American Newspaper

20 January 1944
Thursday night
Part VI

My sweetheart,

Your five-page December 30 letter was something. You are coming up to that number that I write you once in a while. Don't you forget, I thoroughly enjoy reading them too.

I'd like to read Aunt Georgia's poem. How are she and Uncle Rob[27] coming along? I know she has me on her list for not writing her; you know what to tell her, don't you, dear?

You know, honey, I will get a kick out of seeing you in some of the new things you have gotten since I have been away. Darling, it will be so exhilarating to see you again.

Getting my teeth cleaned didn't hurt at all. You see, honey, when you can tell by my writing how I am feeling, it just goes to show how well you know me. Dearest, you do know me very well. Keep on, darling. I want you to know me. That's why I love you so entirely.

I am sure you can write a three-thousand-word short story. All you have to do is keep on as you have been. You can do it. I wish I could offer a suggestion, but you know me.

I love you tremendously,
Your husband,
Phil

P.S. Dear, I love you "a real whole lot." I say that in every one of my letters. I won't ever tire of saying this, darling. Honest, I won't.

---

[27]   This is Aunt Georgia's husband.

20 January 1944
Thursday night
Part VI

Darling Jackie,

In a way, things are critical. The coal strike is responsible for your coal being short. Baltimore will stick on. It is the only city that has its schools open.

Mary[28] is something. No wonder she wants to get married with a guy calling her his darling wife. It's a funny thing, Jack, but all the people in my family can eat, of course including me. I'll admit mine.

OK, dear, I won't worry about you worrying about me. It is now, I know one the ways of feeling toward me. Oh yes, dear, when did you fall in love with me? Did I ever ask you that question before?

Darling, I won't come back wounded. I am coming back just as you sent me, all in one piece.

Dearest, for all the sweet things you say, Jackie, I will always be just as you want me to be—ever yours, your lover, your husband, and everything you want me to be.

Sweetheart, I am madly in love you. I always will be too.

Your husband,
Phil

P.S. Dearest, I love you "a real whole lot." Terribly much.

---

[28]   This is Phil's oldest sister.

21 January 1944
Friday noon
Part I

My darling love,

Today, I got your very lovely two-part Thursday (January 6), Friday (January 7), and Sunday (January 9) letters. My love, your letters really mean a great deal to me. For the last few days, I have been receiving a great deal of mail. Every one of your letters that I receive make me feel more and more happy, darling. Keep on writing, please, your letters to give me inspiration—and that which you say, "that stuff to carry on." Honey, you are so much of me that I hardly know what to say. I know the only way to really tell you. That is to take you in my arms, caress you, fondle you, love you, and let you know this, dearest, is the only way I truly know of letting you know, how I truly feel.

We will be so happy when we are together again, I want so much to talk to you, tell you all the little things which we enjoy listening to each other say.

My arms about you I want to place so much; my lips on yours, our souls burning together their love for each other. I love you tremendously.

Your husband,
Phil

P.S. Darling, I won't forget that I am mad about you. I love you "a real whole lot" always, all ways.

22 January 1944
Saturday night
Part I

My dearest love,

Oh yes, I got a letter from my mother today. Everyone is fine.

You know, I keep thinking that if I didn't get these five letters from you, I'd be an awfully low-feeling individual. Your letters can really make me feel like a million dollars. They are, in a way, just like coming to see you. Darling, don't ever stop writing me. Everything you want to write, do so, because whatever you write will be you, and that's what I want always. You want the same from me, so we'll be even when we both write what we feel and think.

Now dear, that's nothing unusual for you, to leave the price tag on a gift. Are you peeved with me because I said that? I bet you are.

You now, every day, dear, say you are feeling "terribly well." Keep on feeling that way. You know how I feel when that's the way you feel. Dearest, I am feeling fine today too. I rested well from last night's work. So on that score, I can't even complain.

Keep sweet, my honey darling.

Your husband,
Phil

P.S. Dearest, with every infinitesimal fiber of my being, I love you "a real whole lot."
Yours forever.

22 January 1944
Saturday night
Part I

My dearest love,

Today, darling, I was quite agreeably surprised—I got your 8 and 9 January letters. I don't need to say how they made me feel. I was very, very happy. Your letters were brought to me while I was in bed this afternoon. I read them, went back to sleep, and dreamed of us. I need not tell you how much I loved you in my dream for writing me such swell letters. Darling, I love you.

Tonight, I indeed intend on finishing the answering of your letters. For a moment, I had intended waiting until tomorrow, but why procrastinate?

In one of your letters, someone asked you why and how you can home and stayed day in day out. Your explanation was very good. Darling, I do love you so profoundly for storing up your happiness for us. We will thoroughly enjoy it. We will get a great kick out of it, dearest. It's virtually the same thing, love. It's that which is waiting for us that makes this existing possible day in and day out.

Yours always,
Your husband,
Phil

P.S. Darling, I love you. I always will too, Jackie. Dearest, I can't help it. A whole lot.

22 January 1944
Saturday night
Part IV

Dearest angel,

Honey, you sure do make me feel good. That expression is getting hackneyed, isn't it? But nevertheless, you do because every time you say how much my men like me or such and such, I really get a kick out of it. The cards that I sent you that the fellows sent me from India are, as you say, an indication of that feeling. Also, I am glad it makes you happy. All my life consists of seeing how I can make you happier than you are already. Is that OK with you? But truthfully, I wish I could be better. I shall earnestly try to be better toward them though.

Who is Merchant going to marry? Do we or I know her?

Darling, it's not against my faith to wear Psalm 91. I'm sorry I gave you that idea. Ever since you sent it to me, I have been carrying it with me everywhere I go. I have it folded neatly and placed in my wallet. It stays with me all the time. So you see, I'm wearing it, and I am taking a great deal of solace in having it with me and reading it ever so often. You see now, honey, you can stop worrying about that part of me.

Not every star in the sky multiplied a million times can tell the total amount of love I have for you.

Your husband,
Phil

P.S. "Your Guy" says he is mad about you; not only that, but he also loves you "a real whole lot." He said too that he'll always love you. I swear it.

Psalm 91 (King James Version)

1 He that dwelleth in the secret place of the most High shall abide under the shadow of the Almighty.

2 I will say of the Lord, He is my refuge and my fortress: my God; in him will I trust.

3 Surely he shall deliver thee from the snare of the fowler, and from the noisome pestilence.

4 He shall cover thee with his feathers, and under his wings shalt thou trust: his truth shall be thy shield and buckler.

5 Thou shalt not be afraid for the terror by night; nor for the arrow that flieth by day;

6 Nor for the pestilence that walketh in darkness; nor for the destruction that wasteth at noonday.

7 A thousand shall fall at thy side, and ten thousand at thy right hand; but it shall not come nigh thee.

8 Only with thine eyes shalt thou behold and see the reward of the wicked.

9 Because thou hast made the Lord, which is my refuge, even the most High, thy habitation;

10 There shall no evil befall thee, neither shall any plague come nigh thy dwelling.

11 For he shall give his angels charge over thee, to keep thee in all thy ways.

12 They shall bear thee up in their hands, lest thou dash thy foot against a stone.

13 Thou shalt tread upon the lion and adder: the young lion and the dragon shalt thou trample under feet.

14 Because he hath set his love upon me, therefore will I deliver him: I will set him on high, because he hath known my name.

15 He shall call upon me, and I will answer him: I will be with him in trouble; I will deliver him, and honour him.

16 With long life will I satisfy him, and shew him my salvation.

22 January 1944
Saturday night
Part V

My honey dumpling,

You said in one of your letters that one of the nights the moon was not shining in your window because it was snowing. You supposed that I preferred it here because it only rained here. Well, I'd want to have the snow and be beside you looking out our window into the sky filled with snowflakes.

Dear, please be careful, and don't let anyone harm you in any shape, form, or fashion. I don't know what I would do if anything were to happen to you, and I must be able to do anything about it. I don't want to have to start a war of my own because some guy thought he could get away with something. Wherever you go, be well protected so that they don't dare bother you.

It was more than thoughtful of you to purchase that Father John for my father. That's one of his favorite medicines. Really, dearest, you are right in there. You know what I mean, don't you, kid? I love you for doing that.

I know you can well imagine how Edith felt with her husband being home, because just as you said, it was about the same time last year that I came home from school. Love you.

Your husband,
Phil

P.S. Dearest, how can I say it differently? Suffice it to say, I love you. "a real whole lot." Honest.

22 January 1944
Saturday night
Part VI

My beloved wife,

Mom does get around quite a bit now, doesn't she? Her health continues to hold up, doesn't it? Does Mom still persist in reducing?

I should say you had a lot of company with Aunt Cill[29] and the children. It is things like that though that take your mind off things for a while and give you a chance to live again.

I tell the fellows everything you say about keeping their chins up, continuing their good work, and so forth. Of course, they say right back, you just keep <u>my morale up</u> and everything will be swell. Can you do that? I know you can. You must.

It is too bad that Vivian is ill again. I certainly hope she improves soon.

I'm glad Aunt Toots[30] liked the letter I wrote her. Not only that, but I am also glad Uncle Sam[31] straightened out the mail situations sometime. He can get it really mixed up.

Frasks Washington certainly didn't lose anytime. Gloria and Grace, what are they trying to do, have a vacation in mid-winter? Herbie will have another fit if Bertha is pregnant, but such is life.

Sweetie, I am going to close up all of this now by saying, dearest, I love you—now, henceforth, and forevermore.

Your husband,
Phil

P.S. Dear, all your poems at the end of your letters were swell. I enjoyed them much. I love you too. "A real whole lot."

---

[29] This is one of Jack's aunts.
[30] This is another one of Jack's aunts.
[31] This is a common national personification of the American government or the United States in general.

23 January 1944
Sunday morning

My darling wife,

I am starting your letter early because why? I can't tell. I just want to write you. You don't mind, do you, darling?

Sweetheart, as always, I love you. I wish sometimes, dear, that I could say that in a different manner. One of these days, the literary side of me will come out, and I will say that differently.

Dearest, I'm well this morning. I can't complain about anything. Hence, I'm per usual.

I'm officer of the day again, so I missed going to church again. Next Sunday possibly, I will have better luck. It's been some three Sundays since I have been to church now.

At the writing of this letter, the morning mail has not come in yet. I hope though, when it does come in, I will have a letter. I'm greedy, am I not? These last few days I have been having very good luck with the mail. You see how habit-forming a thing can become.

Well, I now just came back with the mail. Only Johnnie got a letter. Hence we will sweat it out until this afternoon.

Well, dearest, I'll close now. I love you, truly, dear.

Yours forever,
Your husband,
Phil

P.S. Darling, I love you "a real whole lot." Honest, I do; can't help it, dearest.

23 January 1944
Sunday evening

My darling beloved,

Honey, I was not disappointed today. I got a letter in this afternoon's mail. It was part II of the 9 January letter in which you had Aunt Georgia's poem. I also got all letters from Hudson. He says India is OK. He wants us to finish here and go over there to help them. May I go? Emphatically, you answer, "No." I agree with you.

Darling, I do wish I were there to help you with the income tax. But that's all right; you can do just as well if not better than I would. I know you can.

With your bond now, dear, in ten years you'll have $6.25 more than you have now. Not bad, is it? I am of the opinion that I will have to get in on this Fourth War Bond Drive with one bond of $18.25. When I get it, I'll send it home to be put with the rest.

Aunt Georgia's poem is certainly worthy of commendation. Tell her for me that I thoroughly enjoyed reading it.

Dearest, keep sweet, because that's the way I love you most. I will always be yours, Jackie, my love.

Yours forever,
Your husband,
Phil

P.S. Dearest, I love you "a real whole lot" forever and forevermore.

24 January 1944
Saturday night

My dearest darling,

These are just a few lines which I do hope will find you so very well. As always, darling, I am feeling just right and per usual, except for being quite beat. It's been a very long day for me.

I did not get any mail from anyone today. I hope I get some more mail tomorrow.

Sweetheart, as always, I am thinking a great deal of you.

Gee, I wish I could think of something to write, but sometimes you run out of things to talk about. That's me now.

Dear, I wish I could hold you in my arms now and tell you how much I love you. Because I do love you, madly. It will always be that way, my dearest love.

Everyone here is OK. The fellas are doing pretty good. They have decided they will continue to do so until everything is finished.

Yours I am forever,
Your husband,
Phil

P.S. Darling, I love you "a real whole lot."

25 January 1944
Tuesday afternoon

My dearest love,

Just what I'm going to write, I can't for the life of me say. I know this though, I could write the rest of this letter by saying over and over again, I love you more and more each time I write it and sincerely mean it, darling. That's the truth, so help me. Do you believe me, honey? I know you do.

I got no mail this morning, but there is mail this afternoon. Maybe I'll have some luck; if not, there is tomorrow.

Today is really a beautiful one, the kind we like. Me, I am per usual, just a bit beat. But with a good night's rest, I'll be, using your favorite expression, "fit as a fiddle."

Dearest, I do hope you are feeling swell too. Are you? You had better be, or else!

Sweetheart, I love you, madly, tremendously, wholeheartedly, truly, and everything that you like, Jackie. No kidding, I really do. Always I will too, dearest. Well, I close the letter hoping that later on today I can think of enough to write again tonight.

Yours,
Phil

P.S. I love you, dearest, "a real whole lot." Really, I just do.

27 January 1944
Thursday night
Part I

Dearest darling,

Really I hardly know just where to start. First I owe you an apology for not having written you yesterday, but I got hung up in some work, so I just couldn't find you a moment even to scribble, "Dear, I love you." But in my mind, Jack, I said it over and over again. Jack, darling, I love you madly; I always will too, my sweet.

As you have noticed, my honey, you see that my unit address has changed. I am now at the 571 Port Company instead of the Co B-484 Port Battalion TC. It's merely the changing of the name.

Darling, I got one of those letters yesterday which you wrote around 12 January which you had put as the fourteenth or the like. Today I got two more dated the twelfth, but for different days today.

As always, my beloved, they make me unusually happy. I love you very much for it, dearest. Keep sweet, darling,

Your husband,
Phil

P.S. Dearest love, I love you "a real whole lot." Honest.

27 January 1944
Thursday night
Part II

My dearest love,

For the last few days, I have been awakening after having thought of you a great deal and wanting you so much that I have felt very much like you have felt. I know it seems paradoxical that we should share the same experiences though we are so very far apart. Darling, I do miss you though; all of my being cries out loud for you so very often that I pray ever that soon we will be together, and forever too, my love.

I want to end those dreams of yours, my love, and be there to turn our radio on. Not only that, but also to take you in my arms and love you as you have never been loved before.

You see now, inasmuch as I know what your resistance needs, as soon I get home, I will know just where to start to build it up. Don't you think that won't be a happy duty for me, Jack? I am almost sure I will cry with joy and ecstasy when I find out I can start to do it. How will you feel, my love?

Darling, don't you worry; we will be happy when we are together again. I'll see to that with the help of God.

Wholly, I'm yours,
Your husband,
Phil

P.S. Dearest, with all my strength, I love you "a real whole lot" forever.

27 January 1944
Thursday night
Part III

Sweetheart darling,

Edith is terribly happy with her husband at home. I know how you feel then, honey.

I thought James Manns was in the army. The way it looks, everyone is really having his or her troubles. We have ours too.

I'm glad you liked that wine Mrs. Gladden gave you. As soon as you drank the first glass, I bet there wasn't an hour before you were dead asleep.

Occasionally, I get around to spending an evening that's rather enjoyable. It does give one a new lease on life. Tonight I saw *Put Your Best Foot Forward*. It was nothing extra, but I really enjoyed it.

It's good that you and Mary can go down to Washington and let that help you to relieve the monotony of things.

Mornings when I come in and before I go to bed, I listen to the radio. The boogie-woogie does make me try to sand and the jitterbug. Can you imagine me doing all that?

I can't exactly say what makes me start my day off decently; sometimes it starts rather rough and a lot of people catch it, but most of them are OK.

Yours forever,
Your husband,
Phil

P.S. I love you—immeasurably too, darling. A whole lot of love is in my heart for you too.

27 January 1944
Thursday night
Part IV

My honey dumpling,

I got a letter from my mother today. Everyone is fine. She said Mary had gone down to see you. It is something that she takes you in her confidence. It just goes to show me what's said that everyone likes to tell you their worries and that you don't have anyone to tell yours to. That just goes to show how destiny is treating you and me. Mary's constant talking of sex to you just means that my mother just isn't telling her much, so she is coming to you. She must be going through a lot trying to figure out what life is all about. You know the score on all the things she is asking you.

Gee, honey, I will be glad to start helping you use those things which you have put aside for us to use. I am glad you liked the towels my mother sent us.

I betcha my aunt Dee[32] talks you to death every time you see her. Want to bet?

I shall be looking forward to James' letter. I know my mother would to see James after his not having been home for a year. I am sure he could have come home before now, but it is just something in him that makes him do things that way.

Yours with all of me,
Your husband,
Phil

P.S. I love you so too, dearest. Also "a real whole lot." Keep your chin up, honey.

---

[32]   This refers to one of Phil's aunts.

27 January 1944
Thursday night
Part V

My angel love,

Did Gloria stay out practically the whole while Basefield was home? At any rate, she did stay out. That reminds me, when I come home, should my leave be for a month or six weeks, you will not teach any of those days unless you want me to be in your class. That, darling, will be done without any argument whatsoever from you. Of course, I know you would do that anyway, wouldn't you? I bet you would.

Jack, that was a task, going to the library for you. Are you going to have me do that again when I come back? I do remember all that thoroughly.

Darling, I'm glad the weather is fine and that you feeling fine in every respect. Keep it up.

I'm per usual. This time a wee bit beat, but other than that, I am OK.

Sweet, I keep thinking of you, wanting you so much. Dearest, I bet when I do hold you in my arms again, I'll squeeze you something awful. You won't mind will you for the first hour, will you?

Dearest, I'll keep sweet for you.

Your husband,
Phil

P.S. Dearest, I love you "a real whole lot." Yours forever, honey—Phil.

29 January 1944
Saturday evening
Part I

My dearest love,

Pardon all that scratching over of the date and days, dearest. My excuse is that I've been planning to use this sheet for all the days you see marked out.

My sweetheart, I wanted to write you yesterday when I really got all your letters and when I was really way up in the air. You know that's where you get me when you write such grand letters. Darling, I love you tremendously for doing that, I always will too. My beloved, plan as though I might, I just didn't take the time to write you. If you don't forgive me, you can spank me whenever you want. I wish it was right now, dearest. I would certainly retaliate with a very tight bear hug.

Along with your letters yesterday, I got a letter from Britt. It says that Clark got to go overseas so very soon after his marriage and that Calloway is now at Crownsville[33].

Your letters were for the 13, 14, 15, and 16. And were they right in there. Don't say a word.

Yours forever,
Your husband,
Phil

P.S. Dearest love, I love you "a real whole lot," as always.

---

[33]   This refers to a former psychiatric hospital located in Crownsville, Maryland.

29 January 1944
Saturday evening
Part II

Honey dumpling,

I am terribly glad that you are feeling so well and that cold doesn't bother you any at all now. Keep up the good strength. Dear, keep on being as sweet as you are, right, now and I will more than just love you—I'll always be every inch of me a part of you, forever and through eternity.

For me, dear, I am OK. I can't complain about anything. I'm per usual. Really I am, darling.

We have passed another week without each other, but we know not too far off in the future, we will be spending all our time together.

I can well understand how you feel about accepting my aunt's invitation for dinner, ok. I do know how you feel about people, so don't you worry yourself about it all. Do as your mind wants you to, and think nothing of it. I won't say a prayer for you to change in that respect, darling. That's a part of you which makes you, so don't worry about it. In a way, I wish I could be the same way. Furthermore, I love you the way you are—that's the best reason why I don't want you to change.

Your husband,
Phil

P.S. My beloved darling, I love you "a real whole lot" truly.

29 January 1944
Saturday evening
Part III

My darling wife,

My sweet, don't spend too much of your time worrying about your shortcomings. The things you no doubt believe to be unbearable are possibly just the very things which make me love you. Then too I could never take it upon myself to tell you what could be wrong with you when there are so many things wrong and seemingly unbearable with myself. There's only one thing I ever want to tell you, Jack: that's how much I love you. Everything I do for the rest of my life will be definitely pointed toward telling you over and over again, dearest darling, "I love you" always. A whole lot.

I am sorry that Mary and you didn't get a chance go to Washington. Maybe later you will get an opportunity. Whenever you to go, have a swell time.

I wonder what the army wants with my uncle when he has the family that he has. I am glad Phil is letting anything slip by him.

Your little poems at the end of your letters are always stimulating. I like them.

Yours, dear,
Your husband,
Phil

P.S. Darling, don't ever forget that I love you "a real whole lot."

29 January 1944
Saturday evening
Part IV

My beloved wife,

Dear, I wish Cill could be right when she says that when you could get mail for several days, someday it will come true your prophecy. You were lazy in not getting up to see how "prophecy" is spelled. Is that correct? I'm too lazy to ask how it is spelled. Which one of us is lazier?

I wanted to see the film *Sahara*. It was here some time ago, but I missed it everywhere. Maybe it will crop up somewhere, and I'll see it. It is supposed to be a good feature, my type.

Darling, I will take your advice and be near a bed when I pass out, else I'd remember to put the covers over myself. Frankly though, I don't intend getting that drunk again as long as I live. At any rate, you know me. I may or may not.

My sweetheart, for what I said about the gift that made you feel down in the boots, I am sorry, because really, I did not intend for it to be that way. I understand everything perfectly, and I do admire you for doing as you did. I love you for it. Please don't worry about it, please. I love you.

Your husband,
Phil

P.S. Mrs. Kane, your husband says "I love you, Jackie." A whole lot. And that he will never stop.

29 January 1944
Saturday evening
Part V

Beloved dearest,

I'd like a little snow now myself. Maybe we might get to sled ride together one of these days, Jackie. I would love that, but I've never been in the daredevil rides that some fellas would take, not me.

Don't you worry, your Luther League program will turn on out. I betcha everything nice. It will with your name the item or thing, and whoever loses will have to produce to the winner the thing within two months. OK?

Dearest, I am terribly and immeasurably glad that you can't drink like I do. Weird to see you that way. I wouldn't know what to do, really I wouldn't. Then too, there is very little of my satisfaction in it. Each time I get that way, I feel quite silly and ashamed of myself to you. Just keep on being Jackie, that's the way I want you and no other way. Finally too, I never feel better, it's usually worse.

The boys are OK. Oh yea, I'll see what I can do about making you dream of me.

Keep your chin up, honey, and keep smiling. I'll be doing the same thing.

Yours forever,
Your husband,
Phil

P.S. Dearest, I am mad about you "a real whole lot." I will be that way always.

5 February 1944
Saturday afternoon

My darling,

I'm just penning this before the afternoon mail arrives. I missed writing you again yesterday. No mail came again yesterday, but this morning, the pamphlets you sent me arrived. I was certainly glad to receive them. Thanks a million, darling, for sending them.

I hope, sweet, that you are feeling like a million dollars. As for me, I can't complain about a thing. Hence, I'm per usual. I am going to stay that way too. You know for whom, don't you? You had better know.

Sweetheart, my thoughts are ever for you. They will always be, my dearest love.

Yours forever,
Your husband,
Phil

P.S. I love you "a real whole lot." Honest.

Thursday night
June 8, 1944

Phil dear,

I caught a nasty cold just as I thought I would. The little girl didn't
have a coat and it was cold, so I had to give her mine last night. Her
sisters said her leg was a little stiff this morning. She did not come to
school. Mom made me take castor oil—as usual. That's right, the chief
reasons why we can't live in Baltimore when you come home. No mail
yesterday or today. I suppose it will be quite slow now with the invasion
on. Received a letter from James today with the nicest picture of him
and one of his friends. I am going to send it to you. It's still cool here.
Hope you are well, Phil. I feel safe now, as though it won't be long now.
I close my eyes often and mentally visualize you at work. With so much
that I could reach out and touch you.

Love,
Your Jack

P.S. It's love, love love.

Jack standing outside her mother's apartment in
Douglas Court in Baltimore, Maryland.

June 13, 1944
Tuesday night

Dearest Phil,

I finished my report cards and all other records today. I'm so glad. Today has been nice, though much warmer. I am most well. No mail today. I have decided to take English 103 and 104. It will help me. They're rather long. The hours are 9-10 to 11-12 to 12:30 - 12:30 to 1. If I can take it, it will give me six credits. I only got 75 from Coppin. With the 9 that I have, it only gives me 84. I hope someone who knows me will take the course too. School lasts from June 19 to the last of July—or did I tell you that once? I hope it will help keep me busy enough not to be wanting you too much. Do you think it is possible? I wonder myself. But at least, the time will go faster. I guess the warm weather is here to stay now. I am sitting on the side of the bed writing this letter, and keep wishing you were lying here giving me one of those soulful and very definitely meaningful looks. You know the kind I mean, don't you?

Love,
Your Jack

P.S. I love you so.

14 June 1944
Our anniversary
Part I (continued)

My darling love,

Dearest, here I go. Today's our third anniversary. Next year, I hope we will be together. I've thought of you a lot. This morning as I slept, I just called out your name, Jackie darling. I love you so much, I want you with all of me. Honest, I do. I wonder if you heard me call you, dearest, through the miles that separate us. Something, dear, I'm sure I heard you. My sweet, with all of me, Jackie, I want you madly. I can't help it, dear, and I won't try to help it because I always want to be completely yours. Truly, darling, that is the truth, so help me.

Forever, I'm yours.

Your husband,
Phil

P.S. Darling love, I love you "a real whole lot." I always will, my sweet.

14 June 1944
Our anniversary
Part II (the end)

My true love,

I hope you will be feeling fine today. You know what I mean, don't you? As for myself, I'm feeling fine, more or less per usual. Can't complain about things too much.

Today, I received my first copy of the *Afro*. I and the fellows got quite a kick out of reading it. Now, if you want, you can hold on to those clippings because the papers have started to come in.

My sweet, I'm just thinking of us—our future and everything. I hope that all this will be over soon and that we can be as we want to be.

Darling, keep sweet always. I will keep all those keeps, dearest.

Your husband,
Phil

P.S. My dearest sweets, I love you an infinitesimal amount—"a real whole lot"—always.

15 June 1944
Thursday night
Part I only

My dearest wife,

My darling, I hope you are well in every respect and that you are not down in the dumps or anything like that.

As for me, I'm per usual. I can't complain about a thing, except that there is that everlasting desire of mine to be always near you. That's a desire, sweets, that I won't do a thing about. Do you mind?

I received today a letter from my mother, the check you sent me from the war bonds, and some very swell clippings. I enjoyed reading "The Spirit" immensely. For all of it, darling, thanks a million. I have a real tight bear hug for you for all that.

Tomorrow, no doubt, I'll get some letters from you anyway. I'm sure I'll have a lot of luck. Sweetheart, I'm forever your one and only. I can't help that be.

Your husband,
Phil

P.S. My dearest, I love you "a real whole lot." Honest, I do, my darling love.

16 June 1944
Our night
Part I only

My darling love,

I received your June 6 letter today. It really was on the ball too. It made me feel as all your letters do. Great from way back.

I'm glad that you are feeling well in every instance. As for myself, I feel per usual. Can't complain about too much; the fellows feel the same way.

Darling, they were very encouraging words, what you wrote in that letter about what we are to expect and do from now until the European war is over. I know it's going to take a lot, but I'll be willing to give, knowing that your love and strength is with me. I can't help but be strong. I do want you to be proud of me.

With every ounce of my strength, I'm completely yours, my sweet love. I'm truly yours.

Your husband,
Phil

P.S. My darling, I love you "a real whole lot." Always, I'm yours.

17 June 1944
Saturday night
Part II only

Darling,

I thought honestly that I had finished for the night, but somehow I want to say something more to you, so here I go, darling. For one thing, I wish that I were near enough to you to say, old lady, I've missed you a lot, but now I have you forever. Honest, I do, darling. Sweetheart, to be able to hold you in my arms close and tight and everything, caress you, bite your ear, and then whisper over and over again how much I think of you—it would be more than sweet, darling. I love you.

My dearest, this summer that faces you, I hope will be one that is full because I don't want you to be worried and all that especially about me. You know, darling, I am keeping all three keeps of ours. I'm not letting a one of them go. A tender, loving kiss for you, my true love always.

Your husband,
Phil

P.S. I love you "a real whole lot" always, dearest. Honest, Jackie. I can't help it, and I won't do a thing about it, my sweetheart.

17 June 1944
Saturday night
Part I only

My sweetheart darling,

Sweets, I hope you are feeling fine and that everything in general is not worrying you too much.

I'm per usual; can't complain about everything, so I'll let it all go. At that, no mail came today, honey, but what did happen was that this morning after I had come in from work and was getting ready to get in bed, I was rearranging my mosquito net, and out fell two letters—one was James's and the other a card that you had sent me from Philly on Memorial Day. I enjoyed reading it, and I also got quite a kick out of reading the letter James wrote me. I shall possibly answer it tonight too.

That day you spent in Philly[34] must have brought back a lot of memories, dear. I keep thinking of the enjoyable time we had there, and I hope that soon we can plan again all those things that will make us happy.

Your husband,
Phil

P.S. Dearest, I love you "a real whole lot." I always will too, my love. Honest.

---

[34]   Philly is in reference to Philadelphia which was part of Phil's territory while he worked for Pepsi Cola.

20 June 1944
Tuesday evening
Part I (continued)

My sweetheart love,

Honey, first I must apologize for not having written you yesterday, but as circumstances would have it, I was caught up so that I just couldn't write you. I will make up for it today, darling. Really I will, sweetheart.

Yesterday, I had some good luck. I received three letters from you, a card from Aunt Dee, and a letter from my mother. The latter folks seem to be doing rather well. Neither of them complained about a thing. Except that they would be glad when I come home. Who wouldn't, darling?

My sweetheart, I'm doing rather well today, per usual. Sweets, I do hope that you are feeling fine, and that too many things are not worrying you. Keep all those keeps.

Your husband,
Phil

P.S. My dearest, I love you "a real whole lot." Infinitesimally yours, my true love.

20 June 1944
Tuesday night
Part II (continued)

My sweet love,

Your letters for 11 June and 12 June were in two parts. As always, my sweet, you know how your letters make me feel. My morale jumped sky-high. Honest, it did, my darling love.

I am very glad, dearest, that you are well and that there are not too many things that are worrying you.

It looks as though you will really take your vacation just after school is finished in July. That is a rather quick turnover. With so many things happening at once, I know that you would be glad for the week to come to an end.

I wonder why she (Martina) doesn't like Philly. I suppose she's just too attached to Baltimore.

Dearest, you are sure having a time with that watch situation. Should you not be able to get a pocket watch, a wrist watch will have to do.

Yours, your husband,
Phil

P.S. My sweetheart, honestly I do love you more than words can say. In actions I want more than ever to prove it to you.

20 June 1944
Tuesday evening
Part III (continued)

My true love,

Honey, I am sorry that I put you to so much trouble trying to locate that type of watch. Honest, I don't know how to tell you I appreciate it. I'm not kidding when I say that, sweetheart. That's the truth. When you receive this letter, if you haven't already gotten it, don't continue to try to get it, just substitute a wrist watch.

Do you think Clif[35] is going to like being in the navy?

Dearest, I am glad that the manner in which I spoke of the invasion made you feel better. Now, don't worry about any part of it, darling. We are going to do all we can to get this over very soon so that we can be together forever. I do pray, my love, that we won't be apart for another summer.

My love, all ways, always.

Your husband,
Phil

P.S. My darling, I love you truly and always, Jackie. I can't help it.

---

[35] This is one of Jack's cousins.

20 June 1944
Tuesday night
Part IV (continued)

My honey dumpling,

Jackie, I'm glad you found your pocketbook, but for the life of me, I can't figure out why they took those letters of yours that I wrote to you. On the other hand, you were lucky or fortunate to have been able to get it.

Honey, do I really have a smooth line of jive? Anyway, darling, I do like talking to you the way I do. How do you feel about it, my dumpling?

Congratulations on those swell grades you got from Prof. Key. That's an average of B for his course. Keep up the good work, my love. I'm certain they didn't make a mistake. My old lady, always remember this: that you can do good because you are the type that knows how to do good. Be always that way, honey, and every day I'll grow more madly in love with you.

Always yours, my sweet.

Your husband,
Phil

P.S. My darling, I love you "a real whole lot." That I always will, my dearest.

20 June 1944
Tuesday evening
Part V (continued)

My darling love,

My dearest, I, like you, hope sincerely that we will not have to write too many more V-mails, but rather, we can hold all these little things until we come home to each other from our days' tasks. Old lady, I do wish I could see you soon. I'd be mad with joy. I might even squeeze you too tight when I hold you in my arms. I couldn't help it.

It's no news to each of us that we want each other very much. That grows too with each day's passing. We won't do anything about it, will we, darling? We want to want each other so very much that we can't do anything but be always ever each other's.

My love, I will keep all those keeps of yours.

Jackie, I'm yours forever and through eternity.

Your husband,
Phil

P.S. Darling, I love you "a real whole lot." I always will too, sweetheart. Honest.

20 June 1944
Tuesday evening
Part VI (the end)

Dearest love,

My master sergeant in one of his few spare moments composed this poem which I think is swell. He's my right hand, so to speak, when it comes to work here. He's right on the ball. You talk about me jiving you, you should read some of the letters he writes his wife. I'm nowhere near him.

I know you wonder why I don't write verses anymore. Can you give me a reason? I can think of a lot of them, but they don't seem sufficient to me, so I won't mention them.

Darling:
You say you are lonely, each time you write,
You dream of me while I sleep at night,
You hope that I'll be coming home soon
And go with you for walks, beneath the moon.
You say you miss me as days go by,
My letters are sweet and yet you cry;

Your husband,
Phil

P.S. My darling dearest, I love you "a real whole lot." Forever, Jackie.

Inscribed on the back: I am a little smaller than I was this time last year. Am I not or is it that these clothes fit me better? This is a step to the office of some of the officers of the area where we stay.

20 June 1944
Saturday night
Part VII

My Jackie love,

Your letter written the day after our third anniversary, June 15, you covered a great deal. I have a lot to be thankful for, dearest.

Those words of yours went profoundly with me when you said you loved me tenfold more than you did this time last year. In every way that my mind can conceive, I will do my utmost to be deserving of that love you've given me. My sweetheart, I'd rather die, and I mean that sincerely, than betray any of the faith, confidence, and love that you have in me.

In the year that has passed, Jackie, you have been able to throw off that feeling of forsakenness that you had. Your letters have given evidence of that. You have kept up marvelously—mentally, spiritually, and physically. We will continue to ask God to let us have each other soon so that we won't have to be so unhappy. We are that while we are apart. Dearest, I love you.

Your husband,
Phil

P.S. Dearest, I love you "a real whole lot." Forever so, sweetheart.

20 June 1944
Tuesday evening
Part VII (the true end)

My dearest darling,

Here's the rest of that poem: Dear, maybe
You think of things in used to do,
And write when often you've feeling blue.
I say to you, "Sweetheart," my love,
It's you, only you, I'm thinking of.
I know you miss me as days go by,
But you cannot be as lonely and
I know what the word lovely means.
And how. I feel from what I've seen;
I cannot make a show or dance
I cannot make dates or have romance,
I have a job that must be done
And will not rest until we have won.
I haven't time for dates or play
You say you're lonely, I stay that way.
I don't need women to give me cheer,
It's your voice, darling, I want to hear.
We sit around and play the blues
And wait to hear the latest news.
When you write, sweetheart, my dear,
You say the things I love to hear
Write to me as often as you can
Because I'm a very lonely man—see above best here.

Your husband,
Phil

P.S. Darling, I'm lonesome as a man can be when I think of the distance
between you and me. It makes me sad and homesick too and brings back
memories of me and you. Yours, darling "a real whole lot." I love you.

24 June 1944
Saturday night
Part VIII

My sweetheart love,

Whenever I have the time, darling, I will write you a lot. I wish that every day I could write you at least seven or eight pages. I suppose you'll be surprised when you receive all these letters.

Why did you underline three children, Jackie? Honey, I will like you being addressed as Mrs. Philip G. Kane.

I won't laugh at your and Cill's "rug cutting." Does Cill dance well now, or is she just learning?

I am awfully glad that you are well, darling; keep up the good work. As for myself, I'm a little beat, but I will catch up on my rest, and then I'll be per usual again.

The night has started to get cool now, and breeze is coming in our tent, a sort of refreshing one. It's not chilly. When I go to bed it will be coming right across me. I should rest rather well. I hope so anyway. I wish I could. I could dream of us again.

Dearest, I'm yours.

Your husband,
Phil

P.S. Dearest, I love you "a real whole lot." I will forever. My darling, nothing can ever stop me. I won't let it, darling.

22 June 1944
Thursday evening
Part I

My darling love,

I did it again, I didn't write yesterday. Just couldn't make it, honey.

But all in all, I was all right yesterday, per usual. Dearest, I hope you were the same. Were you?

Today I received two of the sweetest letters from you. They were for the twelfth of June. Honey, I always say your letters really knock me out, and they do, my darling. I don't know honestly how they make me feel. They are my chief morale builders.

Sweetheart, I am very glad that you are feeling splendid; keep up the good work, won't you? And before you know it, I will be giving you some more days off. You won't mind, will you, darling?

My darling, I madly love you.

Your husband,
Phil

P.S. Dearest, I love you "a real whole lot." With all of me, I do, honest.

22 June 1944
Thursday evening
Part II

My sweetheart,

My pen has run out of ink, and now it's a pencil I'm using. Can you understand what I am writing? Yours came out quite well. In fact, I could read everything very well.

My darling, if there was any way under the sun that I could be there at the end of your school day, I would. That I swear. You really don't know how seriously I mean that. It's a great deal, sweetheart. It's true, it would be a "divine reward" for the two of us.

Honey, I'll help you buy gifts if you're with me. Will you? I bet you will. You are entitled to rest on that proposition. You have bought a great deal of them since I've been away.

Dearest, I'm still completely yours.

Your husband,
Phil

P.S. My dearest, I love you, my sweet love. I always will too, Jackie.

22 June 1944
Thursday evening
Part III

Dearest Jackie,

It didn't take long for Pastor Lewis to get his training and commission, did it? Who is your pastor now, Jack?

That was swell of you to take your kids to the park for their art class. I don't know whether I can draw or not, but some of my first efforts were kept on display at home for quite some time. You know, first grade stuff. My mother was looking at it from the viewpoint of an interested mother. Though I can really imagine just how the kids' drawings are. Sometimes, I bet you wonder just what they were looking at anyway.

Sweets, you're really going a long way out of your way to get that watch. I do hope that you get my letter telling you to substitute.

Darling, it goes without saying how I feel toward you. It's always to be, darling.

Your husband,
Phil

P.S. My darling, I love you "a real whole lot." Forever, completely so, sweets.

23 June 1944
Part I (continued)
Friday evening

Dearest Jackie,

My love, I have just got to tell you this: last night I had the sweetest dream about us. The thing that made it so swell was that I was resting well, and it seemed as though I was hours dreaming it. It in all covered a period of about three days. First of all, I came home to you—in fine shape, strong physically and mentally, just the same crazy guy that left you. The real thing was that I loved you more than ever. Jackie, you were never sweeter in your life. You were so loving, soft, and tender that I had to cry for you. Honest. The whole three days we spent with each other. Would you believe it, we spent most of it in our bedroom. The thing that seemed strange though was that its furnishing was of that walnut veneer-type, the kind you don't like. I kept meaning to ask you why we had it, but I awakened before I had a chance to. I love you, my love.

Your husband,
Phil

P.S. My darling, I love you "a real whole lot." Forever I will be yours. I won't do a thing about it, my sweet, ever.

23 June 1944
Friday evening
Part II (the end)

My honey dumpling,

We went to the movies. I had a swell time holding your hands and trying to make love to you. That's why I forgot the name of the picture. In all, darling, we had a grand time together. I wish I could have written this in the morning, I could have written more in detail. Another strange thing too: Pete didn't even get excited during all that. You don't think he has retired, do you? Or would I know more about that than you? Dear, I am sure that all he needs is just some of newnie[36] attention, and he'll be as active as he ever was.

Darling, up to now I am feeling swell. How about you? I hope you're good too, my beloved. Keep always, sweet, my beloved darling.

With all my might, I am forever yours, my sweetheart. I can't and won't be any other way, ever. Honestly I can't help but be.

Your husband,
Phil

P.S. My darling, as each day passes, I will love you more and more. I can't help but do that, my sweet. Honest.

---

[36] This seems to be a term that Phil and Jack use to express sexual desires and/or activities.

23 June 1944
Friday night
Part III (the end also)

My darling Jackie,

I just had to write you again. I don't know why, darling, I suppose it is just "one of these things." I want to talk to you, darling, some more, you know? I wonder a lot of times if you have changed any in the way you look and walk. I know how you feel and think because you write me a lot, and whether you know it or not, that's how I know.

My sweetheart, do you wear your hair the same way, with just a little curl down near your eye where I used to always be putting one? Did all those pimples from the other week clear up yet? Of course, I know you keep your fingernails even and everything. I'd give anything now to have you put your arms around me, and if you wanted, dig those fingers right into me, anywhere.

Darling, madly I'd be happy if I could whisper in your ear "I love you, Jackie darling." With all my strength, I do, my beloved.

Your husband,
Phil

P.S. Jackie, sweetheart, I love you "a real whole lot." And always too, my love. I can't now well help it. No mail today, dearest.

24 June 1944
Saturday night
Part I (continued)

My darling,

I have just finished a nap now. I feel much better now. I have taken a shower and put on clean, fresh clothes—and dear, I am really quite fresh all over. Now my head is clearer, and now I can write you as I want to.

Today, I received eight V-mail letters from you. Now I know just how I am now. I have been walking on air ever since this afternoon when I got your letters. Darling, your letters were sweet and well—every fine thing, nice. My sweetheart, there are no two ways about it, I just don't know how to tell you how thoroughly I like and appreciate your letters. Honey, if I can ever do something special for you, just ask me, I'll do it. I could just hold you so very close to me. For all the grand things you are.

Your husband,
Phil

P.S. Dearest, I love you with every infinitesimal part of myself. "A real whole lot," sweets.

24 June 1944
Saturday night
Part II (continued)

My sweetheart dearest,

Your letters for the seventh, eighth, ninth, thirteenth, and fourteenth were in two parts, and the fifteenth in two parts.

That day you had with your kids at the park must have been OK. Darling, you are really putting yourself on to do everything you can to make your pupils happy and content. I'm glad you were able to control them without a lot of effort. You know no better than I how fatiguing it can be trying to keep up with individuals.

It was so very nice of you to do all you did for the little girls who fell. I know you must have been tired. You had a rather long day.

Your later letters say that your cold has improved. I'm glad that it ended so soon. You have more resistance than you had some time ago. Then too, I can't say a word, you caught it trying to make the little girl comfortable.

Dearest, forever yours.

Your husband,
Phil

P.S. Dearest, I love you, sincerely "a real whole lot." I will always, sweetheart, and no other way ever.

24 June 1944
Saturday night
Part III

My darling love,

We shall live just as say someplace other than Baltimore. Man, we can do everything we want, just as we want. Where do you think we ought to live, Jack?

I will be looking forward to the photo of James.

This night particularly, dearest, I wish there was some way your hands could touch me. But darling, a lot of times you are with me, your hand in mine. Sometimes, I am so weary, what it takes to fuel all my strength to solve a problem or continue answering questions or make things continue is that staying power of your hand in mine. My knowing that you are ever with me, and that you would want me to carry on. It's in those moments that I know you are with me spiritually, and that being so, your strength gives me ever that desire to let nothing deter me from doing naught else than that which would make you happy and proud of your husband.

Darling, I am forever your lover.

Your husband,
Phil

P.S. With each day's passing, I love you more "a real whole lot." Infinitely, darling.

24 June 1944
Saturday night
Part IV

Darling Jackie,

Truly, darling, I too fervently hope that it won't be long. We will be even happy when we are each other's again.

One day you received eight letters like I did today. I know how you feel, darling.

Your grades in your classes went just as I knew they would. All A's. The same thing will be true of your summer school classes.

You know, out of all our traveling, Annie Laurie and the Alexander are the only ones we really continue to correspond with. Mrs. Kimbrough too. I hope she will like the gift.

Your schedule for classes takes up your morning completely. After you complete summer school, if you could, go to regular school. You could get your degree next spring. But then continuing as you hope, it takes about two more years. While it is more feasible, or which would you want to do.

To get those grades you want, you will be kept rather busy, but there will always be those moments. I know that experience.

Completely yours.

Your husband,
Phil

P.S. My darling, I love you—now, henceforth, and forevermore. Thus I always will, dearest. "A real whole lot."

24 June 1944
Saturday night
Part V

My honey darling,

Jackie, I know exactly what you meant when you said that you wish I were beside you looking in that way—a soulful and very definitely meaningful look. Believe it or not, I have a whole lot of such stored up especially for you. There are so many now that you will probably have to tie something over my eyes to stop me from looking so much.

Yes, I have heard the "G.I." Jive here. It's really a fine program. The fellows like it a lot.

I've had a chance to read about ten pages of *Strange Fruit*. Harry has just finished it and agrees with you. It's here on my desk now. I shall read the twenty-ninth chapter before I go to bed. I'll write you and let you know what I think of it.

Darling, it isn't terrible for you to have read those letters over that number of times when I talked about Pete and his soulmate.

Dearest, your letters do make me feel awfully swell deep down inside. I meant everything I said in my June 6 letter.

Your husband,
Phil

P.S. Pete told me to tell you that he loves his soulmate "a real whole lot" and that she will always be his forever. Honest, always.

24 June 1944
Saturday night
Part VI

Dearest love,

My saying that I will be able to wait for you is ever true; I am glad that I said that, because I want you to know that I am forever completely yours alone.

It is true, darling, that it takes a great deal of strength to be strong, but knowing as you say that the connubial joy that we shall share for waiting will be superbly more than that which the masses of married people have ever known. That must be true, sweetheart: to desire one's lover, for such a long period such as we have, must have its reward. We both have known moments that we wanted each other, and our very soul cried out for our love. Our very bodies ached for just the touch of the other's hand or just a passing glance. Our breaths were short, our minds paralyzed on one thought—we needed each other. Our arms wanted so much to hold each other, our eyes to gaze upon each other. Dearest, all that makes us true, and say, "God you must bring us together soon. We belong with each other."

Your husband,
Phil

P.S. It's funny how my handwriting changes, isn't it? Does it tell you anything, Jackie? I love you "a real whole lot." Always yours, Jackie.

25 June 1944
Sunday evening
Part I (continued)

Honey dumpling,

Today, dearest, my luck continued, and I received those swell playing cards, a *Courier*, your 16 June letter in two parts, and a letter from my mother. Not bad for a day, is it, darling? You know how I feel, don't you, my sweet? I am still like a bird—flying high. After such letters as I have been receiving, Jackie, you know why I write as I do. A million thanks, darling, and as soon as I can deliver them, you will receive a million hugs from me alone. Bear hugs, every one of them.

It's a relief, isn't it, to not be a part of a very exacting job for a few months?

I don't blame Rosalind for going to stay with Carroll this summer. Do you? Or is that a very silly question? Margarite is very fortunate too.

For the cards, thanks a lot too.

Your husband,
Phil

P.S. Darling, I love you "a real whole lot." That is how my love will always be. My true love, Jackie, all mine.

25 June 1944
Sunday night
Part II (continued)

My darling love,

Honey, I sure wish I could be coming to you soon so that you could be wishing for me. Wouldn't it be better together?

Talking of salutations, yours used to be first "Dear Phil," but in the last week, yours have been a number of variations. Now please don't change from what you are doing because I don't know what I'd think if you started to write sugar, pie, etc. Those you use serve the purpose quite well and are very meaningful. My salutations will vary because every time I start a new one, it expresses just how I feel.

Has Catherine turned her mind toward romance and love and marriage yet? Or is she waiting for the boys to come back? Does she still look the same?

I'm glad Grandmom[37] got my letter. Oh yes, that reminds me. Did you ever get back Mary's photo that you sent to me?

Jackie, I love you.

Your husband,
Phil

P.S. With all my heart and soul, I love you, my true love. I may never stop. It's "a real whole lot." I'm completely yours.

---

[37]   This refers to Jack's grandmother.

25 June 1944
Sunday night
Part III (the end)

Sweetheart love,

My sweet, I hope you are continuing to feel very, very well in every respect. As for myself, I'm per usual now. I really feel pretty well. I awoke this morning feeling fine. I went to church too this morning.

I read the twenty-ninth chapter of *Strange Fruit* last night before I went to sleep. Inasmuch as I perused some of the book, from that chapter I got the story, and every character is given a place and just how their relation to the story is too.

I heard of your tornado. Is that the first Maryland has had?

Sweets, tonight is a cool one too. I miss you lot. I want you so much, darling. Madly I do, sweets.

With all of me, Jackie, I pray ever that we will be together soon and then that we will ever be that way. I know we will happy, thus, dearest, I will keep all the keeps of ours.

Your husband,
Phil

P.S. Darling, I love you "a real whole lot." Always. Ray Noble is playing "I'll get by"—I will, darling, when I love you always. That's the truth, so help me, Jack.

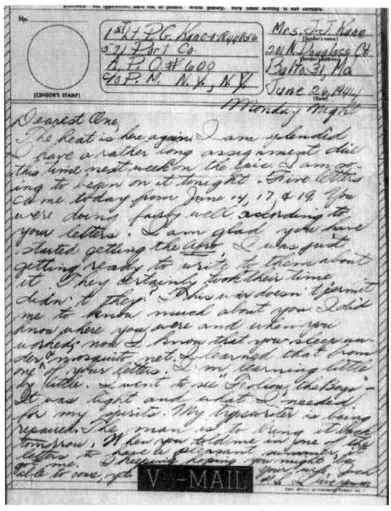

One of Jack's V-Mail Letters

June 26, 1944
Monday night

Dearest One,

The heat is here again. I am splendid. I have a rather long assignment due this time next week on the epic. I am going to begin on it tonight. Five letters came today from June 14, 17, and 19. You were doing fairly well according to your letters. I am glad you have started getting the *Afro*. I was just getting ready to write to them about it. They certainly took their time, didn't they?

This war doesn't permit me to know much about you. I did know where you were and when you worked; now I know that you sleep under a mosquito net. I learned that from one of your letters. I'm learning little by little.

I went to see *Follow the Boys*—it was light and what I needed for my spirits. My typewriter is being repaired. The man is to bring it back tomorrow. When you told me in one of the letters to have a pleasant summer, it got me. I keeping hoping you might be able to come, yet.

Your wife,
Jack

P.S. I love you.

27 June 1944
Tuesday night
Part I (continued)

My sweetheart love,

Hit the bank again today. Guess what? I received ten letters altogether—eight of them were from you, one from my mother, and one from Britt. They all seem to be getting along quite well. Britt wants to go to Atlanta and look that place over. My mother along with the family must be spending her Sundays in the park. She wrote me that that's where she had spent some of her time.

Of course, Jackie, you know how I felt getting all those letters from you. My mail is really coming through now in a big way. I hope yours is too, darling. Yesterday, I also received the wedding anniversary card that you sent me. It carried with it all the sentimental values, fine things, and sweet things you sent me. My darling, for everything that you've done, thanks a true million. You're ever mine, dearest.

Your husband,
Phil

P.S. My darling, I love you truly. "A real whole lot." Forever I'm yours. Always.

27 June 1944
Tuesday night
Part II (continued)

My darling wife,

Your letters for the nineteenth, eighteenth, and seventeenth were in two parts, and the twentieth in four parts. They really knocked me out from way back, my love. I swear they did. I am just floating on the clouds so high. That's the truth, so help me, Jackie.

With your writing me as you have, I've got to say that morale has gone way up. I just don't know what to do or say. Honey, will you keep that up for me? Other than you, your letters come next. And thus they mean everything to me.

Your planning to use your extra time between classes is an excellent idea. You'd be surprised at how much you can accomplish by using that time.

If my mother doesn't expect to hear from John[38] before July, he must have gone a bit farther than England, if there. Do you know where Phil is yet? Or have you told me already?

Sweets, I'm ever yours.

Your husband,
Phil

P.S. With my every breath, Jackie, I love you more and more, "a real whole lot." Honest.

---

[38] This refers to one of Phil's brothers.

Inscribed on the back: The fellow with me is Tom Davis.

27 June 1944
Tuesday night
Part II (the end)

My dearest love,

I'm glad you received the letter telling you about the watch. You know, you sure searched a lot for that pocket watch. For all that trouble, I don't know how to thank you. I sure hope those khaki caps come soon. They'll drop in one, I suppose.

Honey, now, don't let that stuff of research get you scared. For English 103, my research was "Hallucinations, etc." There wasn't anything to it because that wasn't the only one I had to do. Almost every course, I had a required research paper. All you do is pick out something and write on it until you feel you've justified the subject and yourself. Follow the ordinary rules on that part of stuff, and there you are, an A plus. I know what I'd be doing if I were home. "That research paper," frankly it's nothing.

Keep feeling swell, darling. I'm strictly per usual tonight.

Always yours,
Your husband,
Phil

P.S. My darling, I will keep all our keeps and then say I love you "a real whole lot" and mean it.

27 June 1944
Tuesday night
Part III (continued)

My dearest wife,

My darling, I didn't write you yesterday, Monday, but I shall make up for it now.

You know, James really likes to write you and receive your letters; not only that, but he also thinks a lot of you. I don't blame him because I'm crazy about you myself. You've a sweet person, Jackie. There's no two ways about that. That too is another reason why I'll never do naught else but be forever yours.

Those were very thoughtful Fathers' Day gifts. I know they liked them.

Mary Coleman is surely coming on in every respect. But now, I will positively mind, should you try anything like that. Just keep on as we have we'll be where we want, and they will have nothing but respect for us ever. Don't you think so, sweets? My dearest, I'm forever yours.

Your husband,
Phil

P.S. Truly, my love, I do love you "a real whole lot." Completely and eternally.

27 June 1944
Tuesday night
Part III (continued)

My dearest one,

My love, I know that we will and can bear up under our burden with the courage that you give me through your faith, confidence, and pride in me. I can do nothing else but do everything as you would have me do it.

Knowing that you are being brave, strong, ever smiling, and ever true, I will be ever yours, Jackie.

Our keeps, darling, I will keep. I will keep smiling, my chin up, my head up, heart lifted, chest out, eyes ever for you, and heart, soul, mind, and body ever fine for thee, my beloved wife.

Darling, my heart says over and over every day and night, I love you always—"a real whole lot."

Your husband,
Phil

P.S. Love, love, and more love is all I have for you, Jack. "A real whole lot" forever.

27 June 1944
Tuesday night
Part IV

My honey wife,

You know, though, Mom is "right in there" when it comes to putting people at ease during a conversation. Now, she is still suffering with this hot weather, isn't she? Has she lost any more weight lately?

Oh yes, yesterday I got some more clippings, that is "The Spirit," the "News," and the "Sun." You see I had a lot to read, didn't I?

All the fellows' serial numbers who come from Balto and vicinity have 33. It's because the United States is divided into areas. If you don't forget to ask me, I can explain it all to you in detail. Before I was an officer, mine had 33.

Darling, the way I feel, I am certain I could bring your resistance down to nil. Of that I'm positive. We'd both be so very happy doing that for each other, Darling. We will do that as soon as we possibly can. We both would appreciated it immensely.

Yours with all of me.

Your husband,
Phil

P.S. Darling, with all the might of my heart and soul, I love you "a real whole lot"—always.

27 June 1944
Tuesday night
Part V

Dearest Jack darling,

I'm glad you were able to find someone to ride with. I always dreaded that walk myself even if I had to change tires a dozen times, and push the car halfway to school every morning. Oh yes, don't be late for class like myself every day.

Yes sweets, I have had some classes in room 26. I laugh; I can't particularly say where I sat, except on the back row. That was done so that I could lean the back of the chair against the wall and thereby rest better. That position is also an invitation to sleep. Hope I've inspired you with this letter.

Darling, you aren't any sillier than I am. And I'm sure you'll agree that I'm crazy throughout without a doubt. I certainly don't mind your being crazy in the least. Two silly people together make everything come along just right.

Yours always, Jackie.

Your husband,
Phil

P.S. I can think of naught else to say, but that I love you "a real whole lot" always.

27 June 1944
Tuesday night
Part VI (continued)

My dearest love,

I will be most delighted to straighten you out. I need you to do a lot of that for me too, darling. Hence, we'll do it together. We both are out of whack, and honestly, all we need is each other. With that, we can be ever and forever happy.

Rosalind has had luck, but still, if I were her, I suppose I would take a chance. Would you?

Morgan[39] can open your eyes, can't it? I'm almost sure Mr. Davage and Rawlings have their degrees, but maybe they don't. What do you think?

It's almost sure that your Tuesday, June 20 letter was the longest you've ever written on V-mail. It was an excellent four-page letter which sent me in more ways than one. Darling, for that, I am always ever yours. Madly and insanely.

Your husband,
Phil

P.S. I love you so, I love you so "a real whole lot," sweetheart. Forever and always.

---

[39]   This is a reference to Morgan State University.

27 June 1944
Tuesday night
Part VII (continued)

"My wonderful one,"

Dearest, there are no two ways about it, your salutations are coming on. The one I used you used. It's really all right. Honest.

Honey, I don't like to let you know when I am down in the dumps, but then again, if we always know how each of us are feeling, we can be so much more closer to each other. There is no time when I need you more than when I am down spiritually and mentally. To talk to you makes everything a lot better. The same is true with you. That's why regardless of how I feel, I'll let you know. Now, don't ever let me get you down. I know this whenever I'm down. I know you can make everything a lot easier if you were near.

Darling, I hope my mother doesn't tell you too many things about me. You might think you married someone else. I imagine some of things she tells you are surprises.

Your husband,
Phil

P.S. Darling, you know I love you "a real whole lot." This is how my love for you will always be. Forever yours.

28 June 1944
Wednesday night
Part I (continued)

My darling love,

Today, my luck was nowhere. No mail, but why should I complain? In the last few days, I have had plenty of mail. So really, I can't say a word. Do you think I should?

I have been officer of the day today, and it has taken a little out of me, so I can't say that I'm per usual. Honestly I'm a bit beat.

Darling, I do hope that you are feeling fine in every respect. Are you OK, honey? I sure hope that you are.

The weather here is our type—not too warm, just a little cool. The kind in which we can just stay in each other's arms for a long time. That's where I want you to be anyway. When I get there again, that's where you are going to stay forever.

Darling, I love you more than words can say. I do and always.

Your husband,
Phil

P.S. Darling, I love you "a real whole lot." I will always be thus toward you.

29 June 1944
Thursday night
Part I (the end)

My darling love,

Sweetheart, there isn't much that I can think of to write tonight. It's just about the same thing. No mail came today, but again I can't complain about a thing because my luck earlier this week was really swell. But in a way, I can't see why they couldn't have spared those days for me and given me a few each day. What do you think about that?

Darling, I do so hope that you are feeling fine in every respect and that there is nothing at all worrying you in the least. As for myself, I'm doing rather well. I'm not beat, I have caught up on my rest a bit, and now I'm per usual.

Darling, I keep thinking of us and all that. I can't help but want you immensely.

I need you with all of me, sweetheart.

Your husband,
Phil

P.S. My darling, I love you with every ounce of my strength. I love you "a real whole lot." Honest, I do—always.

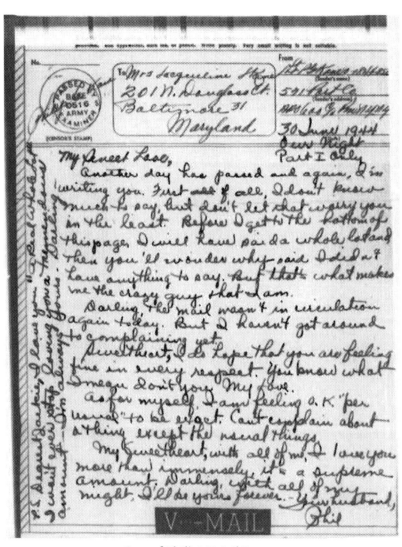

One of Phil's V-Mail Letters

30 June 1944
Our night
Part I only

My sweet love,

Another day has passed, and again, I'm writing you. First of all, I don't have much to say, but don't let that worry you in the least. Before I get to the bottom of this page, I will have said a whole lot, and then you'll wonder why I said I didn't have anything to say. But that's what makes me the crazy guy that I am.

Darling, the mail wasn't in circulation again today. But I haven't gotten around to complaining yet.

Sweetheart, I do hope that you are feeling fine in every respect. You know what I mean, don't you, my love?

As for myself. I am feeling OK. Per usual, to be exact. Can't complain about a thing except the usual things.

My sweetheart, with all of me, I love you more than immensely; it's a supreme amount. Darling, with all my might, I'll be yours forever.

Your husband,
Phil

P.S. Dearest Jackie, I love you "a real whole lot." I won't ever stop loving you a tremendous amount. I'm always yours, darling.

1 July 1944
Saturday night
Part I only

Dearest Jackie,

Here I go again, darling. How much I shall write remains to be seen. Honest, this time I can't think of a thing. Today again, no mail came, but despite all that, my morale is still up. I shall keep it that way, so don't you worry about a thing, dearest. I'll make everything run rather smoothly.

Sweets, I do hope that you are feeling fine in every respect. Are you, dearest? The hot weather and school haven't gotten you down, have they?

As for myself, I am doing per usual. Can't complain about a thing except the usual ones of course.

Sweetheart, keep all our keeps for us. Honey, I am mad about you with every inch of me. I am, my honey love.

Forever yours, dearest,
Your husband,
Phil

P.S. I love you "a real whole lot." That way I will always be, my sweet love. Honest, I will, darling.

2 July 1944
Sunday night
Part I (continued)

My dearest,

I know you are wondering why my writing—that is, handwriting,—was or is as it is. Well, I bought another fountain pen, and it writes like this. Or is it myself who writes like this? I have found out though the type of pen that I can best handle. A lightweight pen isn't much to my hand, and because of that, I am not as steady as I should be. The pen I now write with is rather large. It is the type I have kept writing with for some time now. Which of them do you prefer?

Darling, I hope this will be a very long letter in a lot of parts. You won't mind its being that way, will you?

Today I received four letters from you, and those two very fine caps that you sent me. They are swell, darling. I like them a lot. They look OK too. I am quite pleased with them.

Darling, I'm all yours.

Your husband,
Phil

P.S. Darling, I love you "a real whole lot." I'll always be yours always, darling. Honest.

2 July 1944
Sunday night
Part II (continued)

Sweetheart darling,

With your getting that heavy assignment, it made you think of Coppin[40] again, didn't it, darling? Did it take you a long time to get it done?

Darling, when this damned up emotion and passion of ours one day is permitted to be expressed, we'll be madly in love with each other, so much so that you'll say we're crazy, positively about each other. It is difficult to keep our emotions pent up, but we will be strong because we know that one day, we can express ourselves to each other. Then all of ourselves will be entirely for each other. I imagine that we might frighten ourselves with all our love for each other.

Darling, with all of me I say over again that wholly, completely, infinitesimally, and everlastingly, I will be yours forever and ever, Jackie.

Your husband,
Phil

P.S. My dearest, I love you "a real whole lot." It will always be that way, my sweet. Completely.

---

[40]   This refers to Coppin Teachers College

2 July 1944
Sunday night
Part II (continued)

My sweetheart,

Honey, your letters were from the twenty-third to the twenty-fifth of June. Needless to say, you know how I feel about your very sweet letters. That's what they are, honey. There's no two ways about that. My spirits were made to go very high. So you can guess now just how I'm thinking about you. Gee, old lady, you can really knock me out in more than one way. That's why every day, I grow more madly in love with you. I can't and won't do a thing to help but love you more and more.

My dearest, I am quite glad that you are feeling fine in every respect and that as far as possible, there aren't too many things worrying you, darling. Are there any worries worrying you, honey?

I know how you must have felt hearing from Phil and knowing where he is a relief. It's good that he met up a friend and pal.

Dearest, always you are in my mind.

Your husband,
Phil

P.S. Darling, I love you "a real whole lot." I always will too, my sweetheart. With every atom of me, I will.

2 July 1944
Tuesday night
Part IV

My darling love,

Sweets, sometimes I am dog-tired when I write you. And even though I may say I'm OK, you know exactly how I feel.

There will come a day, dearest, when I will let you do something for my weariness. I know that you will know exactly what to do. Gee, old lady, the thought of knowing that you can make me feel refreshed when I am tired is sweet. Darling, don't think about the past and the things you did that you think made me unhappy; after all, look at all the things that I did that made you unhappy. It's the future now, Jackie sweetheart. We both promise and will do all we can to make our future ever happy and completely in harmony with the world. We will be happy.

With our knowing just what it takes to make us happy, we will hear two doves, madly in love with each other.

Yours, honey,
Your husband,
Phil

P.S. Darling, I love you "a real whole lot." I won't ever forget that that's the way I love you.

2 July 1944
Sunday night
Part V (the end)

My darling love,

That tornado did quite a bit of damage, didn't it? I suppose everyone was quite surprised by it all.

Cill is something, isn't she? What's her idea of calling me a "sweet bunch of sour grapes"? I suppose when I see her again, I won't believe my eyes. Her being so grown up will no doubt seem so unusual.

That salutation was something, darling. It really came on, and I'm not kidding. I don't mind your using it, darling, it's OK.

Things sure will be changed. Does the mayor contemplate making the zoo better than the one in Washington?

I know exactly what you have to do as soon as you finish that letter to me. I'm glad you like that course, darling. Don't let that thesis get you down. There's really nothing to it.

Honey, I'll keep all our keeps.

Your husband,
Phil

P.S. Dearest, I love you "a real whole lot." Honest. Baby, I'm feeling per usual too. Can't complain a great deal about too much.

3 July 1944
Monday night
Part I only

My darling love,

Again, I scribble you these few lines. Darling, I hope you are doing quite well in every respect. Are you, Darling? You'd better be, or I'll do something to you.

As for myself, I am great for a change. I am per usual. In fact, a little better than usual.

Jackie, no mail today, but I did get a *Courier*. I've read it and everything. Enjoyed it. All the fellows are doing fine, none complaining too much.

Honey, I wish I could write you a whole lot tonight. Just can't think of a thing, Jackie.

My love, I love you, "a real whole lot" more than you can think.

Your husband,
Phil

P.S. My darling, I love you with all of me, honest. Sweetheart, I just can't help it.

4 July 1944
Tuesday night
Part I only

My darling love,

Old lady, I love you—"a real whole lot." I wish with all of me that I was with you today. I have marked today. Gee, I wish I could have been with you. I have said that already, haven't I? My love, no mail today, but there's always a tomorrow, isn't there?

With all of me, I hope that you are feeling great and that today wasn't too warm. Was it? It was pleasant for me. I'm feeling just about the same, per usual. You know what that means, don't you, dearest?

All the fellows are not complaining too much about anything.

My sweetheart, I am keeping all my keeps for you and me (us).

With all my strength, I am truly and forever your own always, darling.

Your husband,
Phil

P.S. My darling, I love you "a real whole lot." I will thus all my days. Can't help it, Jackie.

5 July 1944
Wednesday night
Part I (continued)

My dearest love,

Honey, I can't understand it. This pen is the one which, the other night, I complained of its writing not as well as my other pen. Now tonight, there is hardly any difference. Now I have got to admit, it must be myself. What do you think, Jackie? You have some husband, don't you? What on earth are you going to do with him? I'm really interested!

Sweetheart, today I had some luck. I received a letter from you and my mother. It was your 26 June letter.

My mother and the rest are doing rather well. The Japanese beetles are about to eat all her flowers up. Was her flower garden better looking this year than the others?

Always yours,
Your husband,
Phil

P.S. Darling, I love you "a real whole lot." That I never change, dearest. That's the truth, so help me, baby.

5 July 1944
Wednesday night
Part I (continued)

Dearest darling,

Inasmuch as the *Courier* and the *Afro* are published only once a week, they are slow in coming to me. I forgot to tell you, but Monday, I received a *Courier*. I suppose when I get the *Afro* they will all come at once.

I do wish a lot of times that I could write you more in detail about just what I do and how I do it. Right now, that can't be done, but when I can, I will.

I've wanted so much to tell you where I sleep, how I sleep, what I sleep in, and how much I like or dislike certain features of it; where I work and how much I like it; where I spend my leisure and how I treat my men and how we get along. All the things that I know you would be interested in. I'd like to tell you too the little and big things which make me happy and those which make me unhappy.

Your husband,
Phil

P.S. Dearest, with all of me forever, I will love you "a real whole lot," sweetheart. Honest.

5 July 1944
Wednesday night
Part II (continued)

My sweetheart love,

Honey, I am very glad that you are feeling fine in every respect. Keep up the good work. I know you can do it. Do you want to bet about it? Anything you want, and I will give you odds. How about it?

That's tough that heat has come back again. Don't let it get you down, old lady.

From all appearances, your classes are coming along OK. Also your long assignment on the epic is a forerunner of your research term paper. Before you know it, you will have yourself ready. Honest. Honey, if I could write as well as you do, I'd not worry one iota. You've read some of the papers I wrote. Honestly, I believe that you can do a lot better than I ever dared do. Yeah, I mean honestly and truthfully, Jackie. So now, dismiss all your fears. Remember, I know you can do it, so much so that I'm not even worried.

Yours forever,
Your husband,
Phil

P.S. Darling, with all of me, I love you "a real whole lot." Every ounce of me, darling, is all yours forever.

5 July 1944
Wednesday night
Part IV

My honey dumpling,

I can say this though and know that I'm not saying too much that is of military value: I sleep on an army cot, and quite some time ago, I bought a studio mattress that has made my bed soft. By the time I get home, I will have become so used to sleeping in one spot that you'll wonder why I hole up in one place in the bed. But it won't take me long to unlearn that habit. Just let me get home, and I'll prove that to you. Also, I have the reputation of being able to sleep anywhere and anyhow; that is true too. Where you're concerned, I can unlearn that too.

I eat rather well, and I don't refuse anything except beets. I haven't gotten around to being able to eat them yet, hunger or no hunger.

Oh yes, I get plenty of fresh air when I sleep. In all, darling, on that you shouldn't worry about me.

Your husband,
Phil

P.S. My love again I say, I love you "a real whole lot." That's the truth, Jackie dearest, and it will be forever so.

5 July 1944
Wednesday night
Part V (the end)

My darling wife,

Pardon my forgetting to put "continued" on part IV of these letters.

Darling, when I said "Have a pleasant summer," I meant it. Already, dear, you have spent eleven months of your time working hard. Honey, you are entitled to a rest. Inasmuch as you will have August free, why not try to rest a bit? Try a change of scenery. I think some time in New York or a place like that, seeing some plays, the latest shows and movies, would make you feel like a new individual. Don't you think so? Don't worry about the money, just take whatever you need. Let me know what you think about it, darling. If you don't want to do that, what would you substitute?

Dearest, I know what you are saying on account of my saying what I just said. Honey, I am serious, and I do sincerely mean for you to have rest. All yours, Jackie.

Your husband,
Phil

P.S. Every infinitesimal part of me is saying over and over, I love you "a real whole lot." Forever I will, darling. Honest.

5 July 1944
Wednesday night
Part VI (the end)

Dearest Jackie,

In part V I wrote "the end" too, but I think this will be the end.

Dear, I keep praying, and fervently so, that we will be together soon. I too hope that it would be this summer. With God's will, sweets, we will have each other in good time.

The ecstasy that would be ours, darling, truly would be inexplicable. We're to be in each other's arms this summer. The exhilarating joy that would be ours would be nigh or to madness. Darling, the joy'd be ever so thrilling.

Sweetheart, I say that I love you, that I positively will do—not just for now in words, but one day also in my actions. That is ever my earnest desire. Darling, I love you—more than words can say.

Completely yours—forever,
Your husband,
Phil

P.S. Darling, I love you "a real whole lot." Can't and won't help it at all.

13 July 1944
Thursday evening
Part II (continued)

My dearest love,

You know your poems at the end of your letters are always sweet, Jackie. The one on June 27 was short and sweet. I liked it a lot, Jackie.

The sergeant who wrote that poem is quite a character. He has a lot of drive and is considered one of the best stevedores anywhere in our area. Higher-ups have implicit confidence in him. His home is in Jacksonville, Florida. In all, he's quite a fellow. I shall talk about him, no doubt, when I come home.

The typewriter does quite well, doesn't it, since you've had it cleaned? I've never been to Datson's, but if you say it is all that, we'll have to take a moment or so out there.

I do know what you drank while you were there.

Sweets, I'm glad that your breasts are fine and that you don't have to worry about them anymore. I don't want anything to happen to them. You know why.

Your husband,
Phil

P.S. Darling don't ever forget: I'll always love you "a real whole lot." Madly, that way, my love—always.

13 July 1944
Thursday evening
Part III (continued)

Jackie darling,

Freud said a lot when he started that stuff about suppressed desires. Pete got excited this afternoon while I was asleep. Gee, I was angry when I awakened and found that it was not a reality. But honey, I do desire, need, and want you so thoroughly that really there are no words to adequately describe it.

Pete has made a solemn promise that he will do as he knows "newnie" wants things done: "Thoroughly and completely." Just as soon as he possibly can. Then too, darling, I won't let him disappoint you. Because I know you won't let him be disappointed.

Darling, we do need each other with all of ourselves, with all our might. We love each other so much. Dearest, I love you. I love you with all of me. Honey, I will keep all your keeps.

Always yours,
Your husband,
Phil

P.S. How much heavier are you? I've been intending to weigh, but I can't ever think to do it. My love, I love you "a real whole lot."

13 July 1944
Thursday evening
Part IV (continued)

My dearest love,

Jackie, I, like you, wish I could have been there with you after you had bathed. We always got a kick out of being fresh and clean. That day will come again though. We don't have that to worry about.

Honey, I'm glad that you weren't injured when that Mrs. Byrd pulled so like that. Honey, she will get a piece of my mind for having done that.

I am answering your letter from the twenty-seventh of June to the fourth of July; in all, there are eleven letters.

I don't know exactly why I asked you about underlining the number of children. Maybe it was because you were reemphasizing just how many we will have. Darling, any number will be all right, you know me.

I sure wish George[41] had been telling the truth. But I'd been angry too if I'd been in your place.

Darling, I'm thoroughly yours.

Your husband,
Phil

P.S. Dearest, I love you "a real whole lot." I sure hope James[42] does go home; he is the only one who can't come home now just about when he wants to.

---

[41]   This is a reference to Jack's youngest brother.

[42]   James was injured and lost a leg.

13 July 1944
Thursday evening
Part V (the end)

My honey dumpling,

We'll wait then until we're together to decide where we'll live.

I'm glad that you had a rather nice time on the Fourth and that George and Cill enjoyed themselves. You know George and Cill are going to be quite angry with us when I get home and start taking up your time; they won't like it at all.

Sweetheart, I want to write you some more.

The radiance of the beacon—in its disseminating rays—offers a charming and well-lit path for the prodigious amount of love which my heart holds for you.

And so because you are the apex of all things admirable, the zenith of all things zestful, the glory of all things glamorous, the ideal of all things superior, my love for you will flow on a never-ending stream— like the rivers of waters flowing down the sides of a great mountain's summit.

Your husband,
Phil

P.S. I love you "a real whole lot." Always and forever, my true love. Honest.

Sunday night
July 16 1944

Phil dear,

I did the usual today: went to church and Sunday school, went to Mom's, read the paper, came home, took a nap, and then began on my school work. I got quite a bit done today. I guess that guy is going to work us to death for those last ten days. I didn't get time to visit anyone today.

Phil, I have almost worn the pictures out looking at them. You know, I have never seen you dressed like that. They got here fast too, didn't they? They were mailed on the sixth and got here on the fifteenth. I shall be waiting for the others too. In one of the snapshots, the names of the streets had been scratched off. Did you do it, or the censor? It looks as though it is pretty there. I saw Harry rather well too. Was Johnson behind him or in front of you?

All are well here. The day has been sort of humid. I hope you were able to go church today. I should get loads of mail tomorrow from you. How are the boys? Edith's husband is still hanging around here again—been here since Easter. I would have liked to have heard what you would have said tonight if you had been here just a little while ago when I broke the glass of the first photo of you that you gave me. I was trying to kill a mosquito that was on it. You know me and those things don't jell at all. I won't have to ask you to kill them anymore now. I am to see to it now. I shall get a new glass for the frame tomorrow, darling.

"So I find everyone's pleasant spot.
In which we two were wont to meet
The halls, the rooms, and the street,
For all is dark where thou art not."
Keep all the keeps, dear.

Love,
Your wife, Jack

P.S. I love you so.

18 July 1944
Tuesday morning
Part I only

My darling love,

Sweets, yesterday I received six letters from you; and they were grand morale builders. Honest, dearest, I love every inch of you for them.

I haven't written you since last Wednesday. You'll have to forgive me, honey. I just couldn't make it. I know that you will understand. Please do. As soon as I can get straight, I'll write you quite regularly just as before.

My love, I am quite all right. There isn't a thing for you to worry about in particular. Believe me, please.

Jackie, remember always that I love you madly. That completely, I will love you forever—with all my strength. I am forever and completely your one true love. Dearest, I will keep all our keeps. I won't ever have it otherwise—that I swear, Jacqueline. Forever.

Your husband,
Phil

P.S. Darling, I love you "a real whole lot." Every breath that I take is for you, Honey; it will always be thus. Keep sweet.

18 July 1944
Tuesday night
Part I (continued)

Darling dearest,

Would you believe it, but today, I received the clippings that you sent me on June 28. That didn't take too much time. Everything in them was swell. The snap of James was very good. In my opinion, a uniform does something to him. I am sending it back to you by the next mail. But after not having seen him for such a long time, that photo helped a lot. Should he come home and someone take a snap, see that I get a glimpse. Does anyone have a snap of John? I also got the clipping of my cousin. He's grown a lot. The little kids are really coming up so that I will hardly know whether I am coming or going when I see one of them

Dearest, I received no other mail today, but I've read over those letters that I did receive, and I am still up in the air always.

Your husband,
Phil

P.S. Dearest, I love you "a real whole lot" as long as there is a me. I will always be like this toward you, honest.

18 July 1944
Tuesday night
Part I (the end)

My dearest Jackie,

Old lady, I hope you are feeling swell in every respect today and that there isn't too much worrying you. As for myself, I am doing rather well. It's per usual. Darling, my cold has vanished completely. I shall do my best to stay rid of it until I get back to you.

How's your classes coming along? Have you completed your term paper yet? I told you it would not be difficult.

Old lady, remember that I love you with every inch of me. That every atom of me wants you thoroughly and in every respect. Sweets, all of me says over and over again night and day, "I love you, Jackie"—always, always, and always. A million bear hugs for the clippings and everything.

I'm always yours.

Your husband,
Phil

P.S. Darling, I love you "a real whole lot." Every infinitesimal part of me demands that I do.

19 July 1944
Wednesday noon
Part I only

My sweet love,

I have a few moments, darling, and I have just got to tell you that I received the sweetest two letters. They were for the eighth and ninth of July. Honey, as soon as I can, I will answer all your letters in detail. My sweetheart, I am going along rather well, and as far as things go, I'm per usual. Can't complain about a thing. My sweet, I am glad very much so that you are feeling fine in every respect. Keep up the excellent going, Jackie; I know that you can.

My darling, there isn't much that I can think of right now, other than that I want you very, very much. A whole lot more than you realize. Darling, all day, all night, all I do is long for the softness of your embrace, the tenderness of your kissable and ever-loving lips. My sweetheart, I'm always and forever yours.

Your husband,
Phil

P.S. My dearest, I love you "a real whole lot." I shall always. I won't dare but always do so, darling.

19 July 1944
Wednesday night
Part I (continued)

My dearest darling,

Dearest, I am going to try to answer all your letters tonight. I certainly hope that I don't have to get up for anything and that no one disturbs me. I shall keep my fingers crossed.

The letters I received the other day were for June 23 in two parts, July 5 in two parts, July 6, and July 7. The ones I received today were for the eighth and ninth of July.

Of course, as I have said before, your letters do knock me out in every respect. Every time I read them, a new thrill comes all over me. They are so much of you. They really make me feel like a million dollars in every respect. My love, I can't ever stop thanking you for all the sweetness of your letters. They are fine in every respect and always go a long way in making me feel great

Your husband,
Phil

P.S. Darling, I love you with all my heart and soul "a real whole lot." Always, my Jacqueline. Always.

19 July 1944
Wednesday night
Part II (continued)

My sweetheart,

As I write you, my clerk is typing on the same table—not the one who drew our anniversary card, but my other one. Every now and then the typewriter jumps and causes me to sort of mess up this writing, but you can read this, can't you? Darling, I keep saying over and over inside, dearest, I love you "a real whole lot." I wish I were near you forever to hold you tight and close to me. For always, ever.

By now, you know that I have received the caps. For them, thanks a million. For the watch, I hardly know how to say and tell you how much I appreciate your getting it for me. By the last of this month, it will be here. I shall be waiting for it. The probable reason that the smaller packages came before the other is that the small ones get preference.

My every searching glance is for you, Jack.

Your husband,
Phil

P.S. My darling, I love you "a real whole lot." Forever yours I am, Jackie.

19 July 1944
Wednesday night
Part III (continued)

My sweetheart Jackie,

There are a lot of kids at Morgan for the summer. I know it surprises you, doesn't it, that there are so many people who are out for a degree, a lot of them being so much older than we are.

Frankly, dear, in addition to other people being surprised, I too am surprised at my staying overseas for as long a time as I have. It's quite some time when you figure it out.

Honey, I can understand how you feel about being a USO hostess. Knowing you as I do, I know that isn't down your alley at all.

Dear, we'd like to see how that anniversary card took. Could you send it to me so that my clerk and I could look it over?

Darling, I will always love you—completely, never incompletely. I won't permit that to ever happen, that I swear, my darling.

Your husband,
Phil

P.S. I love you. That expression I make often, but each repetition, I mean it more and more, darling. "A real whole lot."

19 July 1944
Wednesday night
Part IV

My honey love,

I am glad that enjoyed your dinner with girls. Tell Catherine I hope she finds the guy she wants, but you should tell her that everything that shines isn't gold, is it?

Sometimes, darling, when I sit down to write, I just can't stop at part III or IV. I just have to keep on writing. You don't mind, do you, dearest? I have to keep on talking to you, darling. I just can't help it, sweets.

Darling, you know I am crazy, don't you? That's probably one of the reasons I said what I did about that research paper. But anyway, I I bet you get an A plus. Darling, you can hold up until the course is over. You are made up of that kind of stuff. So I don't worry at all. Honey, you can't wish I were there any more than I do. I'd be willing to do all your research too, every bit of it.

You know, my mother writes me and tells me that she has plenty of time, but I know it takes some of her time to take care of the baby. But such is life.

Always yours,
Your husband,
Phil

P.S. Every evening's setting sun marks the end of a day in which I have loved more than the day before. "A real whole lot." Always I love you, Jackie.

19 July 1944
Wednesday night
Part IV (continued)

My honey dumpling,

I am glad that all of them, my family, is swell. Has my father predicted the day for the end of war yet? Oh yes, it's been quite some time since I asked about Pop[43]. How's he coming along?

My mother is about right. If the children are like the older ones of us, that puppy won't be there for any length of time.

Who is this instructor that is so near a hoodlum? Do I know him? I am sorry that you have an instructor like that.

Ethel Dorsey, I can imagine, is giving that preacher a real going over. It's funny how old men carry on, isn't it?

No, I don't think anything is going to happen because Phil wrote you. Maybe it's his conscience catching up with him. You know how that is.

Dearest, things are happening among the married folk there. I know Fisher, Bertha's friend. I imagine Mrs. Jennings is satisfied now that she has her two sons free again.

Cill I know is running her block, there are no two ways about it.

Always yours,
Your husband,
Phil

P.S. My every heart's beat is eternally saying I love you "a real whole lot." Always and forever, my darling love.

---

[43]   This refers to Jack's father.

19 July 1944
Wednesday night
Part VI (the end)

My darling always,

The salutations in your letters are really coming on now, dearest.

My darling, I know how you must feel—with every ounce of your strength saying over and over again, we want each other. We need each other, truly. How much longer can we carry on like this? But we can be strong because we know that we have all the faith under heaven in each other. Along, we will keep all our keeps because knowing that we have been strong will just make our love more pure and sublimely beautiful. Always and ever, darling, I am and will be completely and totally yours alone.

With God's help, we will be together soon. He won't have us endure any more than we possibly can.

Remember, Jackie, I am yours.

Your husband,
Phil

P.S. Darling, the more frequently I think of it, the more I know that I can't not ever love you. "A real whole lot." Always, dear.

20 July 1944
Thursday morning
Part I only

Dearest Jackie,

It is quite early as I start to pen you these few lines, but dear, I have just got to talk to you. And what about? The same thing. Nothing in particular. Sweets, I've been thinking of you all morning—over and over again. I keep saying, "Jack, I love you. I always will."

Honey, I feel rather well now, per usual. You know how that is, don't you, old lady?

Dear, I know you are well and feeling fine in every respect. Keep up the good work, honey.

Darling, I love you "a real whole lot." Always.

Your husband,
Phil

P.S. Dearest, I love you forever with all of me. Honey I will keep all our keeps.

20 July 1944
Thursday morning
Part I only

My dearest love,

My sweet, I intended writing you last night, but I fell asleep before I got to writing you. I am making up for it now.

Darling, no mail came yesterday, but there's today. Honey, you are thoroughly correct, I am spoiled so far as your writing me is concerned.

I am feeling well in every respect per usual. I know you are feeling fine too.

I know that the only thing wrong with us is that we miss each other a lot. We know one day that we will be together forever for each other.

I am always yours.

Your husband,
Phil

P.S. Dearest, I am mad about you. I love you "a real whole lot" forever and always, darling.

20 July 1944
Thursday noon
Part I only

Dearest,

I'll have to admit that I am a bit spoiled when it comes to getting mail regularly. This morning no mail came, so you know how I feel now, but there is always this afternoon and tomorrow.

I know you think I am crazy, but I am, so what? Whenever I have a few moments, I just have to write you. That's the way I have of trying to ease up a little.

Darling, don't ever forget I love you. Do I say that often, my darling? All I want now is to be with you so that I can prove to you that I do love you through deed and action, and not just telling you that. Honey, I mean all that I say. That's the truth, so help me, Jackie sweetheart.

Your husband,
Phil

P.S. Darling Jackie, always you are in my heart "a real whole lot." That I mean seriously, sweets.

20 July 1944
Thursday noon
Part III (continued)

Dearest love,

I had some excellent macaroni the other day, and it's been ages since I had any oranges, but I will catch up on them later.

Dear, I'm glad that you have a mind to take a vacation. I'm not afraid of your going alone because you have done quite a bit of being alone, and you know what to do. I know now that you can take care of yourself. Then too, you can come and go as you like, when you like. That would help make things enjoyable for you. When I come home, dearest, we will have a grand vacation together. We'll do all the things we've been wanting to do for such a long time.

It's swell that you girls get an opportunity to have your Saturday night get-togethers.

Dear, I'm glad that you liked the snapshots. I wish I could send you a lot of them. We really put on our "mean strut" later. The censors must have scratched out the streets. Johnson was in front of me. I haven't had a chance to get the other photos developed yet, but as soon as I do, I will send them to you.

Yours forever,
Your husband,
Phil

P.S. You're always mine; I love you "a real whole lot." Edith's husband really gets to break. I wouldn't have said much if I had seen you break that photo. Honest.

23 July 1944
Sunday night
Part I (continued)

Jack dear,

You must forgive me for having skipped again, but it's something I couldn't help. Am I forgiven?

Today, my love, I received four letters, two from you and one from Mom and my mother. They were swell. Mom said despite the hot weather there, she wasn't complaining. My mother expects James home by the last of the month.

Your letters were for the tenth and eleventh of July.

Of course, I don't have to say how much your letters meant to me. I enjoyed reading every part of them. Darling, always your letters help my morale immensely. I have a million fine bear hugs for you too.

Always yours,
Your husband,
Phil

P.S. Darling, I always will love you "a real whole lot." Forever.

23 July 1944
Sunday night
Part II (continued)

My beloved wife,

Darling, I will be glad when those hot days have been finished. I know how they make you feel. You don't appreciate that in the least. That I know.

Old lady, I know what it must have meant to you to have come home and bathed after being a bit fatigued. Darling, I do wish I could have been with you and helped you bathe. I haven't too long ago cleaned up myself and put on some clean clothes. I feel rather well too, dearest.

I bet now you are beginning to complain about the irregularity of the mail just like I was about the first of the month.

Dearest, I will keep being all the fine things you think I am. Believe me. I won't disappoint you. That I promise, my darling.

Your husband,
Phil

P.S. Dearest, I love you "a real whole lot." It will always be there, my sweet. I know naught else to do.

23 July 1944
Sunday night
Part III (continued)

Dearest darling,

Honey, whatever may confront me, I won't let it get me down. I'll do just as you say, "Keep all the keeps of ours."

Jackie, I can well imagine how detestable that fellow must be. I'm glad that you don't have but a few classes to attend. He is everything you say he is and then some. But certainly he is detestable.

Does Hurtle think or know that he is going overseas? It's down his alley to marry one of that type.

Now the thing to do is not to worry about the watch. It will do just like the caps, no doubt. The wrappings on them were comparatively new and had not been opened. In other words, it was all right.

I am a bit funny when I say that our zoo is like the one in Washington. In fact, that is stretching things.

My darling, I'm completely yours.

Your husband,
Phil

P.S. My darling, I love you. Honestly more than you think. "A real whole lot" always, my sweetheart.

23 July 1944
Sunday night
Part IV (the end)

My cherub,

I keep thinking of us so very much, just the same as you do. The past summers we have spent together. I know this summer being different from the rest has made things seem quite different. Darling, I ask God with all my might that we might soon be each other's. Dear, our love needs the immediate presence of each other in order that we know all over again all those little things which go for the making of a complete and full life. One day, again, that must be ours, God willing. My sweetheart, we will keep ever demanding God to help us.

With all my strength heart, body, mind, and soul, Jackie, I will love you truly, forever and through eternity.

Every inch of me is yours.

Your husband,
Phil

P.S. Dearest, I love you "a real whole lot." Totally, I am yours, my sweetheart love.

27 July 1944
Wednesday morning
Part I only

My darling Jackie,

Sweetheart, I just had to scribble a few lines to you this morning. I can't really think of a lot to say, but honey, I want to just talk to you. It's the same old story.

Dearest, you know that I love you, "a real whole lot." You know that I always will too. There are no two ways about it, sweetheart.

My sweetheart, I do pray that you are feeling fine in every respect. As for myself, I'm per usual. Dearest, I am really all right. Honey, don't worry about me because I am all right.

Dearest, I am always yours. I will be that forever, always yours.

Your husband,
Phil

P.S. My darling, I love you "a real whole lot." Always and forever, every part of me is yours.

29 July 1944
Friday morning
Part I only

My dearest Jackie,

Jackie, again there isn't very much to be said; I can't think of a great deal to say.

My darling, I do pray sincerely that you are well in every respect and that you are feeling swell. I know that your sessions at school have finished with today. In a way, you are glad that school is over. Dear, I hope you do take a vacation or something that will take your mind off things for a few days or so. I wish I could suggest something definite. Darling, I wish I could be with you. I know that anything we would do together would make us both very, very happy.

My love, I'm feeling per usual. I can't complain about a thing. Honey, you are always just where you should be—with me, right in the shy heart. Dearest Jackie, that is where you will forever be.

Sweets, don't let anything get you down. Darling, please don't. Remember always, my sweetheart, that I love you madly, completely, and everlastingly.

Your husband,
Phil

P.S. Darling, I love you "a real whole lot." Always, sweet. I will love you always.

30 July 1944
Sunday noon
Part I (continued)

Darling,

In a way, I have a lot to write you, so I shall write small. I do hope that you won't have any difficulty reading all of this.

Yesterday, Saturday, I wrote you a letter in which I called yesterday Friday. I'm forgetting the days. What are you going to do with me, darling? That just goes to show you how I'm doing.

I got quite a bit of mail, dearest: two sets of clippings, a birthday card from you, a letter from Phil, a letter from Annie Laurie, two letters from my mother, and from you eight letters. They were from the twelfth to the eighteenth.

Dearest, there is no need of my explaining to you how they made me feel. Darling, I'm deeply grateful for all that you've done. Honey, they made me feel like a million dollars. A million hugs to you, Jackie dearest. Naturally, I got a great kick out of reading all those letters. My morale is really unusually high. It was quite some time before I got mail this week, and I didn't complain too much, did I?

Yours forever,
Your husband,
Phil

P.S. Dearest, I love you "a real whole lot" always. Your card to me was sweet. I liked the perfume. My mother is OK. Annie L. is in Gary with her sister. Phil is doing all right.

30 July 1944
Sunday noon
Part II (continued)

Dearest Jackie,

Darling, I am glad that you are coming along very well and that you are feeling fine in every respect. You will keep on being that way, won't you, sweetheart?

All the fellows are coming along rather well. They don't complain about things. Oh yes, the card you sent for the Fourth of July came too. Tell Cill I saw where she wrote her name. Tell her I said hello.

Gosh, old lady, everything has gone beyond being sky-high. Just how does one get along with everything costing so very much? You have a right to raise the dickens with all that. I'd rather be with you. Honest, I would.

Darling, I hope you get my letters regularly, because you are just like myself when you don't get any mail. You don't like it at all. We'll both keep our fingers crossed and hope for the best.

Tell Phil that as soon as I get the time, I will write you. I will love you forever.

Your husband,
Phil

P.S. Dearest, I love you "a real whole lot." Always, dear. I had laugh when you said I could go to sleep anywhere. That's a fact, and I do swell specific times. Don't you too?

31 July 1944
Monday noon
Part IV (the end)

Dearest Jackie,

I got up in the front of those photos because that is the way they were taken.

That's tough about William Redmond. Dear, I won't forget that perfume.

Dear, I know that in a way, you are wondering how I am coming along. Hell, as far as things go, I'm doing per usual. I can't complain about a thing.

My sweetheart, I'm madly in love with you. I won't ever be otherwise of that, I swear.

Darling, the day will come too when we are once again in each other's arms; we will say together, it was tough waiting, but we know it was worth it. Don't ever forget, darling, I will love you alone forever. I will keep all our keeps too. I just can't help it, my darling, because with your love, I can do naught else. Completely yours forever, Jackie.

Your husband,
Phil

P.S. Darling, again, I say I love you—most completely and "a real whole lot." Honest. Give my love to everyone.

31 July 1944
Monday evening
Part I only

My darling wife,

Honey, there isn't very much that I can think of saying. I haven't received any mail today. But why should I complain after all the mail I received the other day?

The other day I was going through my things in a sort of lightening of all the things that I have to carry. One of things that went were over five hundred of your letters; I wanted to reread them, but I knew if I did, I wouldn't get rid of any of them. Somehow, I got around to burning them. That really hurt me though, because you have written me many very beautiful letters.

Sweets, I hope you are well. Keep that way. I'm per usual in every respect. My heart, mind, soul, and body are ever yours. It will be thus forever.

Your husband,
Phil

P.S. Dearest, I love you "a real whole lot." Every ounce of me says over and over again, I'm yours forever.

1 August 1944
Tuesday noon,
Part I only

Darling,

I bet you are wondering why it is that I write so many of your letters at noon. It just happens that I can be free at that time, so I scribble you a line or so.

Again, dearest, I don't have a lot to say, it's just about the same old thing.

Jackie, I miss you more than words can tell. I do hope that we can be together soon. All the time I think of the little things we have done together and wish like everything that we will have an opportunity to do all those things again. Darling, God must hear our prayers. They are ever ascending toward heaven, ever supplicating for our being together.

I'm well, dearest, per usual, and I hope that you are doing the same.

Completely yours,
Your husband,
Phil

P.S. Darling, I love you "a real whole lot." I will always be thus for you. Forever through eternity.

2 August 1944
Wednesday morning
Part I only

My darling Jackie,

I have a few seconds to spare, so I'll drop you these lines.

Darling, there isn't much that I can say. I do know this though: I can't recall when I have turned and twist as much as I did last night. Darling, every time I awakened, it was you I was yearning for through and through, my sweets. We will be so very happy when again we can hold each other in our arms.

My love, I am yours always. I'm per usual. I do hope that you are likewise. I will keep all our keeps forever.

Your husband,
Phil

P.S. Darling, I love you "a real whole lot." Always yours.

3 August 1944
Thursday morning
Part I (continued)

My beloved darling,

I just don't know where to start because I have a lot to say, and I don't have a lot of time. Whatever I say, sweets, I hope it tells you just what I want to know.

Dearest, I got from you yesterday three of the sweetest letters I've gotten in some time. My sweets, I'm mad about you for having written them. They've said a lot to me about us. Darling, I got your letters last night, but it was so late that I didn't write. I got three from you, the nineteenth and twentieth, one from my mother who is well, and one from Agnes[44] who told me all about her son Paul and supposed that I knew about him. I shall write her as though I didn't. I got one from Aunt Alice[45] and a set of clippings from you. I had a big day. All of me, darling, belongs to you.

Your husband,
Phil

P.S. Dearest, I love you "a real whole lot." I won't ever forget that, dearest.

---

[44]   This refers to one of Phil's sisters.
[45]   This refers to one of Jack's aunts.

3 August 1944
Thursday morning
Part II (continued)

Sweetheart darling,

My love, I'm glad that you are coming along rather well in every respect.

Your literature assignments were, I can see, a definite headache to you. I certainly hope that you don't have that instructor again for a long time, if ever again.

Darling, I am glad that you're getting my letters. Honey, when I miss a day or so, you know that if I could write, I would. Any time I am free enough, darling, I will write you if it just a line. When you don't get a lot of mail from me, just say, dear, that it's on the way. I know just how you feel when you don't get a letter. I know that you know how I feel.

Dearest, I don't know who the plagiarist is. Maybe it's that guy in India.

My every breath is ever yours.

Your husband,
Phil

P.S. Darling, I can't ever stop saying I love you "a real whole lot." Always.

3 August 1944
Thursday morning
Part III (the end)

My darling wife,

Honey, I too will be glad when I don't have to be tired and weary. I live only for those days. At times, I'm rather beat, I won't kid you. Sometimes I have to drive myself to do all that is to be done.

Darling, the reason I said so much about your accident is that it could have been more serious. Dear, whatever else should happen, please tell me. I'd tell you. Honest, I would.

Jackie, I'm per usual. My feet are coming along fine. I cleaned up a bit this morning—a shower and everything. I put plenty of foot powder on my feet. I have cramps only when I am on my feet for long periods of time.

I certainly hope James does come home as he is planning. Thanks for the commentating, Jack.

Your husband,
Phil

P.S. Darling, I love you "a real whole lot." I will do that forever and through eternity, my sweetheart.

Inscribed on the back:
Taken in North Africa. Not so long before I left for the Invasion of Southern
France. Do you think my clothes are too small or was I just naturally fat or
should I say stout? I almost have a bay window. The cap I's wearing is one
of those you sent me. I like them, I think they look alrite. How about you?
The tent door which I had the snap taken is the same type which I lived with
Johnson and Carpenter. It was just like this one. Am I still a mischievous boy?

Inscribed on the back: This officer is my company commander. Just recently made Captain. I'm sorry I was standing too far out of the sun. The house behind me was in our area. I didn't get a chance to stay in it. I was sleeping in a pup tent then. The fatigues I wear a lot because they take dirt and somehow save on laundry.

Wednesday October 18, 1944

Diary dear,

Today has been one of those rush days when it was all that I could do to keep pace with myself. To me, it's fun to have days like that every once in a while. It helps to keep my mind off things that it shouldn't dwell on, if I am to be reasonably content. Mom looked exceedingly pert today, and I wouldn't be surprised if she didn't "spring" a second father on us. You know how mothers are sometimes about things like that.

Thursday October 19, 1944

Diary dear,

A six-page letter came today from Phil. I was happy. I have read it many times.

I missed taking some notes in my grammar class today by watching the young married couple who are also taking the course. They were writing notes to each other and smiling after they had written them. They are quite a handsome, though childish-looking, pair. I wonder how it feels to sit in a class next to your husband.

Wednesday October 25, 1944

Diary dear,

How can some days do it, go by so uneventfully? As I look back, I cannot recall anything unusually good, unusually bad, or unusually unusual happening. It was a lovely day too and would have lent itself nicely to a grand occurrence. The brief, informal discussion in our creative writing class of books and their authors was interesting and quite meaningful.

Thursday October 26, 1944

Diary dear,

No letters came again today. It's odd how letters can mean so much to a person, especially in times like these. A friendly letter—just some paper with some writing on it,—a message, most of the time insignificant and unimportant in content to all but the receiver, yet many persons are sad because they did not get one, or many a life brightened because they did get one. I wish I had gotten one today.

Friday October 27, 1944

Diary dear,

One has to be most careful about the people to whom he talks and what he says to them. I casually remarked to a young lady student that the hour in one of our classes on Thursday had been boring and that I thought one male student asked entirely too many ridiculous questions. Today the student to whom I referred in my conversation overtook me as I walked to the bus and said, "So I bore you in class." I was shocked. I did not go out to Morgan to make enemies. I am only too glad that this student was not a girl, as I doubtlessly would have had an enemy. I know now what to say and what not to say to that young lady who misconstrued my remark.

Saturday October 28, 1944

Diary dear,

My tailor has had some most interesting experiences, some of which he related to me today. He learned his trade in Jamaica and came to the US to practice it. His first work was with several large tailoring firms in New York City. He wanted to go into business himself, but found competition in New York too great. As a result of this and some marital trouble that resulted in a divorce, he came to Baltimore to establish himself. Now he has a continuously growing trade and needs assistance. He can find no experienced colored person; he can find no inexperienced colored boy who would be willing to work as an apprentice. He does, however, have an experienced white tailor who is willing to work with him, but only under the conditions that the business shall be in the white man's name. Such is life!

Monday October 30, 1944

Diary dear,

I visited my mother-in-law today. She is a most likeable person and not at all like the stereotypical mother-in-law that one hears and reads about so often. Her chief desire seems to be in seeing Phil and me happy. She has spent a happy life with her husband and wants all her children to be happy with their mates. Should I ever have children and live to see them wedded, I hope that I will be like Mother Kane.

Wednesday November 15, 1944

Diary dear,

Received two snapshots of Phil today. He looks wonderful. I thought, "Here I am worrying myself to death about him, nerves worn to a frazzle, and he's over there looking disgustingly healthy."

We have been married for three Christmases already, and not one of them have we spent together. The first year he was in Georgia, the second year in North Dakota, and the last one in Africa. I hope this year he won't still be in France, but will be here instead. I wouldn't ask for anything else.

Monday November 20, 1944

Diary dear,

I wrote nine letters today. They were all in answer to letters that I had received. Receiving letters is grand, but oh, the task of answering them! Maybe I won't have to do that anymore until Christmas. Here's hoping I won't!

November 23, 1944
Thanksgiving Day

Diary dear,

It wasn't hard for me to determine what I have for which to be grateful. There is so much. Yet I am not happy. Deep inside, I am miserable. I thought that by going out to school this year and by being around so many youngsters who take life so lightly, I would feel less unhappy. Now I don't think I do. As long as I am in a class, I am all right. But as soon as it's over and my mind is unoccupied, I go right back to that empty, desperate, longing feeling. I wonder how much longer I—and hundreds others like me— must endure it.

Saturday November 25, 1944

Diary dear,

I went to camp today—the first time since Phil left over eighteen months ago. As usual, the soldiers were numberless. I met one of the commanding officers. Trying to get across the bench at the table without exposing too much of me was really a problem. Dinner was delicious. Much sand sought refuge in my shoes. After being unsuccessful in blowing up my dress, the wind did succeed in blowing my hat away. Ten (I guess) soldiers sped to get it. It was fun watching a group of recruits, who were letting the onlookers know by the quality of their marching that they were "green."

25 in Port Unit Honored for Service in No. Africa

By MAX JOHNSON

AFRO War Correspondent with U.S. Troops in Eastern France

[Copyright, Reproduction in whole or in part expressly forbidden.]

WITH INVASION FORCES IN SOUTHEASTERN FRANCE (By Cable) — The First Legion of Merit awarded to a member of his race on this French front went to M-Sgt. Samuel J. Washington, 35, of Orangeburg, S.C., member of a port battalion unit on duty in the Marseilles area, while twenty-four others in this outfit received Purple Hearts as a result of injuries.

Washington's citation was given for outstanding service in North Africa, where he was stationed from May, 1943, until shortly before the Southern France invasion. It read in part:

Leadership Praised

"For exceptionally meritorious conduct in performance of outstanding service in the North African theatre of operations from June 1, 1943, to April 15, 1944.

"During this period Sergeant Washington's energetic leadership as stevedore foreman was directly responsible for raising to a high degree the standard of efficiency shown by his outfit."

A former Allen University student, Washington has a mother, Mrs. Julia Washington, in Orangeburg, and a wife, Mrs. Mattie Washington, in Jacksonville, Fla. A brother, T-4 James P. Washington, also is serving with a port battalion.

Purple hearts were awarded

(Continued on Page 5, Col. 1)

25 in Port Unit Honored

(Continued from Page 1)

members of Washington's outfit, who were injured by shrapnel when some thirty Nazi planes attacked their ship on August 16, while unloading 400 heavy ammunition. Pvt. Ivey J. Ward, 27, of 334 W. Fifty-third Street, NYC, and a soldier from Louisiana were killed in operation.

Pfc. Emmett W. Yancey, 36, of Rochester, N.Y., was the lone Westerners among those receiving Purple Hearts, and 2nd Lt. Leonard Grant, Cleveland, Ohio.

the only officer. Others, all of whom have recovered from various wounds are:

LOUISIANA—T-4's Willie Hawkins, Norco; Alonzo Sanford, Slaughter; Cpl. George Span, Jackson; Pfcs. Joseph Wilson, Plaquemine, Jimmie [...] Francis, Emanuel Smith and Paul Smith, New Orleans, Davis Porter, Tangiphaoa; Samuel Joseph, Alexandria.

GEORGIA—T-5 Frank Allen, La-Granite; Pfc. Seth Tatum, Gabbettville.

TENNESSEE—Pfc. Baggard Johnson, Shelbyville.

FLORIDA—Sgt. David Bythewood, Jacksonville; T-4 Arnett Burnett,

Tampa.

TEXAS—T-4 Elliott Friday, San Antonio; S-Sgt. Robert Haynes and Cpl. George Davis, Houston; Pfc. John Johnson, Austin.

This outfit, activated at Indian-town Gap, Pa., in December, 1942, has been overseas eighteen months, serving mostly in North Africa.

Unit Has 16 Officers

It has sixteen colored officers, more than any other such outfit in Southern France.

Two Baltimoreans in the group are 1st Lt. Philip P. Kane, 1630 E. Chase Street, a 1941 Morgan graduate, whose brother, John (Sugar) Kane, is an ex-Morgan athlete now on duty on the Normandy front, and 2nd Lt. Harry A. Carpenter, Jr., 1730 N. Carey Street, former city school teacher.

Other Easterners among the unit's officer personnel are:

First Lt. Roland R. Milton, 524 T Street, Northwest, Washington; 2nd Lt. William M. Overton, 2463 N. Twentieth Street, Philadelphia; T. Nathaniel J. Hurst, NYC; 2nd Lt. Frank R. Lawton, Jr., Brooklyn, N.Y.

First Lt. Robert H. Holloway, Chicago, who commands one company in this outfit, is the first officer of his race I have seen on this front in such a position.

Thursday, December 7, 1944

Diary dear,

It is three years today since the attack on Pearl Harbor. Many radio programs included the song – "Remember Pearl Harbor", as if so many hundreds of us will or can ever forget it when we think of the moments, the hours, the days, the weeks, the months, the years of unhappiness and heartbreak that that attack has resulted in for us.

I can remember December 7, 1941 as though it were only yesterday. It was Sunday evening, and Phil was home on a weekend pass from Fort Belvoir, Virginia. We had been reading the Sunday papers. When the radio program was interrupted by the startling news of the Pearl Harbor disaster, Phil turned and looked at me and said, "Well, Jack, there it is, and there goes our hopes for being together for a long, long time."

No, I'll never forget Pearl Harbor.

Sunday December 10, 1944

Diary dear,

For a long time, I have been trying to think who Miss Jones, our writing instructor, reminds me of, and this afternoon, coming home on the bus, I thought of who it is. It's Elisabeth Bergner, the star of the play The Two Mrs. Carrolls, which I saw during the summer. The two do not have the same facial features, but both have a certain gentle air about them. The two of them are petite, fragile, Dresden-like creatures.

It's grand not to have to think of school for a long time. I have just finished looking through my snapshot album. I wish I had not now. It is such a silent reminder of yesterday's gaiety with one who means so much to me. Oh, for even the promise of a glorious, happy tomorrow!

Inscribed on the back: Another snap dear. I wish I could step out of this photo into your arms. You know that would make me most happy through and through. It would.

May 29, 1945
Monday night

Darling,

The weather is the same, and so am I. All are getting along nicely. I got all my invitations for graduation addressed, mailed, and delivered personally. Now that is out of the way. I also went to see a sick church member. I was up to see Mother and Dad Kane. He had some corresponding that he wanted me to do. I will get on it tomorrow. Mother Kane let me read the letter that you sent her for Mothers' Day. It was such a nice one too. She said that she was going to always keep it. I also read some of John[46]'s letters, and one from Thomas[47]. I have a little trouble reading both of their writing. John seems to think that he will be coming home soon. Your mother was writing to Thomas. She gave me a very good picture of Thomas. He had it taken the last time that he was home. Your father told me to tell you that he is tickled to death with his new eyeglasses. He says that he is like a child in that he writes on everything now, every chance that he gets. He tried on my glasses while I was there. But mine are not strong enough.

He is going to try to make arrangements to get Mother Kane out to commencement. If he can't, he is coming himself. His car is still not running. I didn't know that Frank[48] had sold his car. Your father asked me if I would mind if they came out in Irvin's[49] truck. I had to laugh at that one.

Ally[50] walked part of the way home with me. You know he is the man of the family now, next to your father, with all the rest of you gone. Your mother said that Mattie[51] had brought the best report card home, better than any of you had ever had. That's swell.

---

[46]   This refers to Phil's brother also known as "Big George"
[47]   This refers to another of Phil's brothers.
[48]   This refers to one of Phil's uncles, his father's brother.
[49]   This refers to another one of Phil's uncles on his father's side.
[50]   This is one of Phil's brothers.
[51]   This is one of Phil's sisters.

Your May 20 letter came today, and you were still getting along all right too. I am glad, dear. Phil, you know that your birthday is near. Please tell me what you want as a gift. Please, Phil. You know, you never do this for me. Won't you do it just this once for me?

Love,
Your Jack

P.S. I love you so.
P.P.S. I shall love you forever.

Inscribed on the back: This photo was taken about the first of June in our battalion area. It was a sort of cool day, that's why I had on my trench coat on. The rest of my outfit is pink. This is the uniform I wear when I go to sit on the General Court Martial Court. This is a little French auto beside where I am standing.

Port Battalion Has Best Food in Marseille

By OLLIE STEWART

MARSEILLE, Aug. 6—En route to Marseille by train, I met Lt. Roland R. Milton, of Washington. He not only shared his rations with me but uttered the following words of warning and wisdom:

"There isn't much to eat in Marseille and what you get in the mess will probably leave you hungry. So, remember the 484th Port Battalion. We feed better than anybody in town."

How right he was! But what with visiting the staging areas and talking to soldiers in other units, I didn't get around to the 484th until the end of my stay in this crowded port. I went out on Sunday, with the girls on the Canebiere Red Cross staff.

Had Fried Chicken

Yep, they had fried chicken—and plenty of it. Hot rolls went along with the Gospel bird. And the meal ended with two helpings of home-made peach ice cream. Frankly, I didn't believe it, but everybody else said it was true, so I'm setting it down as Bible truth.

The battalion was housed in a series of stone buildings known as the Abattoir, or slaughter house. Cool in the summer because of the rocks, the outfit is and has been comfortably set up here for months and does not expect to be sent to the Pacific. The men have made an impressive record for themselves, handling cargo that arrived from the States.

It seemed to me that the presence of a large number of colored officers had a tremendous effect on the attitude of the men. I didn't notice the resentment that is always present when white officers are in charge of colored soldiers.

Capt. Holloway Commander

Capt. Robert H. Holloway, Chicago, is the only colored company commander. Easily approached, respected, Holloway talked with me at length about the post-war period in America and what it will hold for all of us.

"These men here now will be very impatient with things as they were before the war," he said seriously. "To ignore them will be criminal as well as dangerous."

Lt. Philip (Killer) Kane, 1630 East Chase St., Baltimore, kept bringing Morgan College and football into the conversation. "The Bears better be good this fall," he stated. His fellow Baltimorean, Lt. Harry A. Carpenter, didn't have much to say. He had to get back to his work on the dock.

Virginia Represented

Virginia was represented by Lt. William D. Kendall, 11 E. Clay St., Richmond. Then came Lt. Leonard Grant, Cleveland; Lt. Nathaniel Hurst, NYC; Lt. William Johnson, Chicago; Chief Warrant Officer Albert L. Carter, Kansas City, Kansas, and W/O Charles Duncan, Philadelphia.

In the enlisted men's club I was surrounded by soldiers from Baltimore and environs. Cpl. John N. Brooks, 1015 Brantley Ave., was the spokesman. He was in charge of the club and was taking in money with both hands as the thirsty soldiers jammed the bar. Before the war, Brooks had a grocery store at Fremont and Lafayette. He has lost 71 points but isn't too much worried.

Band Plays in Marseille

Cpl. Francis Chase, Westminster, Md., has 70 points and heads a G.I. band that plays for soldiers in and around Marseille. He had a band in Baltimore, and went to Vocational. Now he wants to get back to civilian life and organize another orchestra.

Also from Westminster is Cpl. Francis Brooks. Sgt. Charles Dowdy used to live in Sparrows Point. T/Sgt. William Fisher and Pfc. James N. Brown, Sr., are from Baltimore. Brown is the busiest boxer in Marseille, a featherweight.

Pvt. Thomas B. Brown, 2109 N. 18th St., and Cpl. Gerald Pote, who once attended Shaw University, are both from Philadelphia. They didn't have enough points to mention the subject.

Await Ride Home

However S/Sgt. Clarence Ivory, 89 points, and Pvt. Thomas C. Torregano, 89 points, both from New Orleans, are sweating out a ride home.

Others seen include Cpl. Fred L. Williams, Jr., NYC; 1/Sgt. Richard E. Rice, Omaha; Pfc. Wright Cesseaux, Tampa, Fla., and Sgt. Vincent Smith, NYC.

Published in Baltimore Afro-American, August 25, 1945

11 September 1945
Tuesday evening

My darling Jackie,

Just about noon when I received two of your regular letters—for the first and second of September and some clippings. Your letters were swell. They put one on pins and needles. Honey, they made me feel swell all over.

Sorry, honey, that it is so hot there now. You know, I could use some of that weather with you. Right here, it's first warm and then cool. Today, it's warm. The nights are cool however. That's not bad at all.

Mail really piled in on you, and you had a lot to answer.

Sweets, I am well, I will stay that way. You need not worry. Please don't because I will do all that I can to be always just right for you, my dumpling.

Truly, when I think of you and coming home to you and holding you in my arms, I am thrilled all over. Sweets, I just close my eyes and think. The glory of being with you, of having you close to me, darling, is an ecstasy. To have you in reality is enough to make me want to just stop living so that I could hold that moment forever.

My dearest love, we will both faint when we are together again. I know that we will be so thoroughly happy. Madly happy.

Now, J. J. Kane, my hair does stand at attention when I think of your running your fingers through the hair on my chest. I will prove it to you when I come home.

Honey, I sent you some more perfume today. I hope you will get it soon. You, I hope, will like it. It's a little different from the other. But I think you will like it. I am sure we can come to some agreement about dancing close to each other. I recall that dance in Norfolk too. Remember how you said if I did any jitterbugging, you'd stop and leave me right in the middle of the floor? Remember?

Dear, I have a lot of memories—a million of them about us. They are what keep me going. I treasure them because they are a part of you. They put you in my mind for the ages, for which I will love you.

Dearest,

I wish I could be sure of the date exactly. But already, I've seen officers get right on the ship and then get pulled off to stay behind for some reason or the other. That has happened to some as many as three times. Sometimes one wonders. I keep hoping that everything will be all right.

Honey, I am holding out for a trip home before Christmas. If I'm not by then, I swear that I will be a disappointed and hard-to-get-along-with individual.

I hope they, NYU, won't wait too long before they send that letter of acceptance.

Take it easy, old lady. Don't you go to see things that will make you lose your sleep. I'm the only guy who is supposed to make you lose sleep.

Honey, I will keep my hopes exceedingly high. We will have all that we have waited for and wished for.

Sweets, I know how you felt with everyone enjoying themselves and you being alone. Sort of reminds you of those days when I used to be working and you were waiting for me. Gee, honey, I do so want to make up for that and the loneliness you are now a part of.

15 September 1945
Our night
Part I (continued)

My darling,

Just where shall I start your letter? Really, I must say I don't know exactly where. I don't have a lot to tell you. It seems that for some reason, the mail has started to hold up for a few days. I suppose it will be coming through all right rather soon.

Dearest, I hope that you are still splendid and as swell and as fit as a fiddle. Stay that way, please, my dumpling. You will, won't you, my beloved dearest?

Darling, I am per usual and all right. There's nothing except this waiting to complain about. I do my share too, old lady.

Your husband,
Phil

P.S. My darling, I love you "a real whole lot." Always and forever.

15 September 1945
Our night
Part II (the end)

My sweetheart darling,

I want to talk to you some more, that's why I had to write you this
part II.

Honey, I want to tell you that I miss you madly. That as long as I
live, I will have to be near you. I will be holding you tight and close to
me. Squeeze you something awful, Jackie.

My dearest, all of me is thoroughly and completely yours. I don't
want myself to be any other way. Honest, I don't, my old lady. I won't
be any other way.

Darling, I will keep all our keeps—every one of them.

Always yours,
Your husband,
Phil

P.S. My dearest, I love you "a real whole lot." Forever and ever.

16 September 1945
Saturday night
Part I only

My dearest Jackie,

Where should I start my letter to you? Well, sweets, I don't know of a lot to say.

I'm per usual and all right. Really I am, darling, and I am going to stay that way for a long, long time.

My darling, I hope that you are swell and splendid. You are, aren't you?

Today, I had court again. It did not leave me morose as some of these cases do.

I felt well enough to enjoy quite thoroughly a stage show of Block and Sully. They are quite a team.

Dearest, I am still quite mad about you. Sweets, I will always be yours—heart, soul, mind, and body

Your husband,
Phil

P.S. My dearest, I love you "a real whole lot." Forever I am your love, your Phil.

Inscribed on the back:
The fellow with me is the defense counsel for the General Court. A very good lawyer, he wins a lot of cases. He's from Chicago. A very interesting fellow. He wants me to study law. He thinks I've good head for the law. What do you think? Always your, Phil.

Inscribed on the back:

This is taken on the main street of Marseille. I was on my way to court to get transportation to go to camp. That is the Court Martial Manual in my hand. The fellow with me is a Criminal Investigation Agent. I just happen to meet him a few minutes before this photo was snapped by a walking photographer. How do you like it of?

That shirt I have on is one you sent me. It fits o.k.

See those hairs bulging out of my collar. They just waiting for you to run your fingers through them. They miss you so much. As much as I do, dearest.

17 September 1945
Sunday night
Part I only

My darling,

Right after I came from church this morning—oh yes, I was late again—I found four V-mail letters waiting for me. You know how I feel, don't you, when I get a hold of them? They were what I needed, dearest, to make my day complete. They were right on the ball. I will answer them through a regular letter. They were for the fourth, sixth, eighth, and ninth.

Darling, I'm fine. I will stay that way too. That way I will be, forever and ever.

As for you, stay as sweet as you are. Always, I will be completely and forever yours.

Stay and keep as sweet as you are, darling. As for me, I will be all that you want me to be too. Always.

Your husband,
Phil

P.S. My darling, I love you immensely, "a real whole lot." Always your lover, my Jackie. Always.

17 September 1945
Monday night
Part I only

My darling,

My sweetheart, I have missed you so much. I don't know how to say just how much. But it is more than I know how to say it.

Darling, today has been sort of warm, but not too much.

I am well in every respect, per usual, and all right. You know I will stay that way. Just for you, Jackie.

Dearest, I wish and hope that you are doing fine in New York. You know, everything splendid and fine.

Sweets, keep sweet and swell in every respect. You know I am going to stay that way forever. Always and forever.

Your husband,
Phil

P.S. Darling, I love you "a real whole lot." Yours, dearest, I am.

18 September 1945
Tuesday night
Part I (continued)

My dearest,

Today I received your two regular letters for August 30 and September 5. Dear, you know how they made me feel. Sweets, I do mean that a great deal, that they made me feel great all over.

You know, Jackie, I am glad that you liked those photos. I have another on the way, plus some perfume. I hope it comes through soon too.

Darling, I did feel pretty after that rest. It is just as I say—missing you is my greatest trouble.

The watch you sent me, dearest, is working fine. Honest. I have a new chain for it. In all, it's going good.

Always your lover,
Your husband,
Phil

P.S. My darling, I love you "a real whole lot." Always your sweetheart.

18 September 1945
Part II (continued)
Tuesday night

My dearest love,

The papers were the *Stars and Stripes* and several French magazines. It's OK. I suppose about French, I can read it much better than I can speak it.

I eat at an officers' mess when I am downtown on the court.

In fact, then, darling, we will both profit—I by experience and you by reading. Together we can go a long way. Don't you think so? I don't think I will be ahead of you in the least.

Sweets, I won't even forget that we are entirely each other's in a supernatural manner. Thoroughly we are each other's. That's the way we will always be.

Forever yours,
Your husband,
Phil

P.S. My dearest, I love you "a real whole lot." Forever your Phil, I am.

18 September 1945
Tuesday night
Part III (continued)

My darling,　-

Dearest, I'm per usual and all right. I will stay thus too, my dear. Honest, I will. I know naught else to do.

Sweets, you stay the same way, please. Jackie, a lot of the fellows are supposed to go home. Carpenter, Hurst, Johnson, and Scott are supposed to leave about Sunday for the States. They have a lot of points. None of them except Carpenter or Hurst have less than eighty-nine points under the old score. Now, long after they leave us, when they will be home is the question, but I don't suppose that it will be long. I know you are wondering when I am coming home. Darling, I do wish I knew. Really, I do, my dumpling. I will have the company after Hurst leaves. What comes after that, I really don't know. The army has me covered, as they say!

Your husband,
Phil

P.S. My dearest, I love you "a real whole lot." Always I am your lover.

18 September 1945
Tuesday night
Part IV (the end)

My dearest love,

Honey, I wish I could be sure of our having a swimming pool. We want that. Then you can swim without thinking of what people will think of how you look in a swimsuit.

I read the clipping to my friends—that is, my men. They got a kick out of my being called "Killer[52]."

I hope your address will come soon. I want to write you as soon as possible. Tell me everything.

Darling, I love you madly. I will always and forever be your true lover. I want to be always yours. I know that you will let me be your lover and husband.

My dumpling, I will keep all our keeps. Every one of them.

Your husband,
Phil

P.S. My darling, I love you "a real whole lot." Always and forever yours.

---

[52]   This nickname was given to Phil by his brother-in-law, Phil, after a character that appeared in several Tom and Jerry animated films in the early 1940's that after several name changes became Spike Bulldog. (Source: https://en.wikipedia.org/wiki/Spike_and_Tyke_(characters))

19 September 1945
Wednesday night
Part I only

My darling,

My sweets, I do hope that you are quite well in every respect. I am doing the same as usual. I am per usual and all right. I will be thus always and forever.

My dumpling, you know that I am still missing you terribly. I won't ever stop, my dumpling.

Dearest, I wish I were right beside you, my Jackie. Right now, I'd give anything to be in your arms. To hold you close to me and tell you just how much I love you.

My Jackie, I am keeping every one of our keeps—all of them.

Dearest, I'm madly yours—forever and ever.

Your husband,
Phil

P.S. My darling, I love you "a real whole lot." Always and forever.

20 September 1945
Thursday night
Part I (continued)

My dearest wife,

Guess what? Today I received a great many newspapers, those two fine shirts that you sent me, and your regular letter for the thirteenth of September. Sweets, you can imagine how they made me feel. The shirts are swell. I like them a lot. They are of a better quality than the others, though not as cool. In all, they are swell, and thanks a million for going out of your way to send them and to find them for me.

As for your letter, Mrs. Kane, it got right next to me. A little more, possibly, than the usual letters do. I don't know exactly why, but that's what I felt about your letter. Dearest, as I write, I will endeavor to tell you why.

My dearest, I do love you sincerely.

Your husband,
Phil

P.S. My dearest, I love you "a real whole lot." Always and forever I will love you, Jackie.

20 September 1945
Thursday night
Part II (continued)

My dearest love,

Your letter was written exactly one week from today. Now we are seven days and twenty-four hours closer to each other than we were last week. Darling, I pray ever so fervently, frequently that we will be each other's very, very soon.

My Jackie, I am so very glad that you are finding things pleasant for you in New York. It's "nice" that you enjoyed the show at the "Apollo[53]."

Honey, see, I wish I could have sat beside you and helped you read that book. That would have been real good to have done. That brought back to me memories of one Sunday when we drove to Druid Hill Park and sat and read.

Your going to the automat[54] really brought back memories. Recall how we gained all that weight by eating there?

Your husband,
Phil

P.S. My darling, I love you "a real whole lot." Forever, I am your one true lover.

---

[53]   The Apollo Theater is located on 125th Street in Harlem. Both the interior and exterior of the building were designated as New York City Landmarks, and the building was added to the National Register of Historic Places. (Source: https://en.wikipedia.org/wiki/Apollo_Theater)

[54]   This refers to the Horn and Hardart Automat in New York City which was a cafeteria that featured prepared foods behind small glass windows and coin-operated slots.

20 September 1945
Thursday night
Part III (continued)

My dearest darling,

Honey, I'd better be among those men who have been sent back before Christmas. Nothing in any way could be more pleasing to us than to be each other's before Christmas. In fact, as soon as possible would be a billion times better. I wish I could say that now I am coming back to you. That would be great, very much so.

These years of separation have made us appreciate our wanting each other very much, my darling.

I did not have any idea either that it would take so long. Think, darling, four years it will be next thirteenth of October. That's a long time—in fact, too long. Especially inasmuch as we have not spent a lot of it together.

Always your love,
Your husband,
Phil

P.S. Always I will be yours "a real whole lot." Truly, Jackie, I love you.

20 September 1945
Thursday night
Part IV (continued)

My dearest old lady,

My love, faith, with my being completely and madly in love with you, has made me keep you in my heart, soul, and mind. Always, in my waking hours, in my dreams, even in my most sound sleeping, you are present.

Untold joy awaits our first embrace, all of ourselves will flow to each other in an even maddening stream of ecstasy born of our love, a love which has languished for ourselves for so very long.

I can well imagine, my darling, how you slept. We've both spent many restless nights trying to rest. All we needed was each other. Thank the good God that those moments when we can be each other's are close at hand. We will sleep the sleep of lovers from henceforth.

Your husband,
Phil

P.S. My darling, I love you "a real whole lot." It's not just a little either— it's all of me.

20 September 1945
Thursday night
Part V (the end)

My love,

Have I told you that since the points have been recomputed, that I now have ninety points? I sure hope that they mean something to me in an immediate sort of way.

You know, the way you said that you spent your day made me think of how in a way you were lonesome. A lot of times I too have been so alone. I wanted you through and through. That's why I am worrying anyone and everyone who can give me some way to get to you soon.

Darling, I love you more each day; with rising of the sun, my heart swells more with love for you. With the rising of the moon, I love you more. Hence, each day's passing finds me more yours than ever.

Always with all of me, I'm yours.

Your husband,
Phil

P.S. My darling, I love you "a real whole lot." Always and completely.

21 September 1945
Our night
Part I (continued)

My beloved wife,

Today again, I had excellent luck in that I received three letters from you and one from my mother. That's not bad. They were all V-mail. Your letters were those that I missed. They were for the tenth, eleventh, and twelfth of September.

My mother said that everyone was well at home. She was sort of glad that all the children had gone back to school. It means for her a little rest. It was always sort of funny when I was at home. My mother really was glad to have school open so that she wouldn't have to be worried to death by us.

Darling, your registering—and its taking you so much time—must have been a bit fatiguing.

Dear, I do pray that everything will go very well for you. I sincerely mean that, Jackie, my love.

Your husband,
Phil

P.S. My darling, I love you "a real whole lot." Yours with smothering of me.

21 September 1945
Our night
Part II (continued)

My darling wife,

Every time I think of you, dear, I will say a prayer for you. Remember, Jackie, spiritually I am beside you. Any of my strength which I can give you is all yours—every bit of it, my sweets. In fact, all of me with everything that is me and mine, is yours. I can well imagine that you were disappointed in not being able to attend the day classes and thereby receiving more credits. But with your determination so do well and everything, I am sure that you'll make the day classes. In fact, I am positive that you will.

Their allowing you thirty-eight credits only, does that affect in any way what classes you may take or the length of time it might take to complete a prescribed course? Honey, I know I am asking a lot of questions. I'll stop.

Your husband,
Phil

P.S. My dearest, I love you "a real whole lot." Forever, dearest, I will be yours.

21 September 1945
Our night
Part III (continued)

My sweetheart,

I will be waiting to write you at your next address.

Honey, get a room that you will like and one in which you will be secure and in which you won't have to worry about a thing.

In the letter last night, I spoke of your being a bit lonesome. In your letter from the eleventh, you said that you were lonesome. Darling, I do wish I could do something about it. Would that right now, I were with you.

Darling, I'm per usual and all right. You know I will remain that way for a long, long time. Really, I will, dear.

I am sorry about your having caught that nasty old cold. You know you won't have it long. You'll throw it off in no time.

Now, honey, don't be too far up on the movies. We won't have any to go to when I get home.

Your husband,
Phil

P.S. My dearest, I love you "a real whole lot." Forever I am yours, Jackie, through eternity.

21 September 1945
Our night
Part IV (the end)

My darling,

You know I want to sit beside you and hold your hand a lot. Really I do, Jack.

You can pretty well imagine how all the fellows are feeling as they are getting their orders sending them home.

Dearest, I love you so much. I want so much to tell you over and over again how much I do love you.

My sweets, would that I could entwine my fingers in yours at this moment, walk beside you, gaze into the sky, bump against you intentionally or accidentally, all that would make us both happy, I know.

Darling, I know you think I am crazy. Well, I am about you. I always will be too, dearest, for ages to come.

My sweets, every inch of me is you.

Always your lover,
Your husband,
Phil

P.S. My darling, I love you "a real whole lot." All of me says over and over again, I do.

September 22, 1945
Sunday night

Dearest husband,

Another Sunday has gone, darling, and I am glad. You know why I am glad too.

I went to church this morning, ate dinner at the Y., came home and read the papers, wrote some letters, went out again room-seeking, ate a light supper at the automat, and am now in bed preparing to go to sleep—if I can.

You know, I have found out that there is something in the subways to which I am allergic, and which causes me to go into fits of sneezing. Isn't that a mess? I suppose I will have to stick to the streetcars and buses. That is, if the drivers of the latter don't strike. There is talk of it. The elevator operators go on one tomorrow. Workers at Ford Motors are on a strike, as well as the delivery drivers in NJ[55], plus many others throughout the country. It looks as though now that the war is over, our internal strife is beginning very intensely.

I have felt very lonely today. It seems years and years since I've seen you, Phil. I look at other women and young girls with their husbands and boyfriends, and envy them right out. And I'm always seeing something to remind me of you—big red apples, the *Pittsburgh Courier*, a lieutenant, a rickety old automobile, a brown-striped bathrobe in the store window, a Pepsi-Cola advertisement, etc. All these just keep the wound raw.

I hope you were able to go to church today, dear, and that things are going along just as you would have them to. Keep well, darling.

Love,
Your Jack.

P.S. May ours always be one mind with but a single thought—to be always each other's.

---

[55]   New Jersey

22 September 1945
Saturday night
Part I only

My darling love,

My dearest, another day has gone past, and I am without you. But we are twenty-four hours closer, and that is a lot. I pray that there won't be many more of such hours.

I hope that everything has gone along with you quite well, my sweet.

As for your husband, he's per usual and all right. He's going to stay that way too.

I worked again in court. It was not so depressing.

Again, dearest, I just keep hoping that before many moons, we will each be in the other's arms.

Always, I'm yours.

Your husband,
Phil

P.S. My darling, I love you "a real whole lot." Always I'm your lover.

1 October 1945
Monday night
Part 1 Maybe

My darling,

My sweetheart, I received your letter regular for the twenty second of September. Darling, I'm glad that you are feeling great. Stay that way, my darling.

Your letter found me feeling "per usual" and alright. I will stay that way for you always, my dearest.

Sweets I do pray that not for many more Sundays without you. I want you so very much. All of me cries out for you through and through.

Dearest that's something you being allergic to the dust in the subway. How are we going to ride downtown when we get together?

I read about those strikes folks are going on back there. I hope they make up their minds before I get back.

Honey, I know how you feel. I am feeling the same way with so many fellow going home. Darling, it can't be long. It can't be.

Always, I'm forever yours.

Your husband, Phil

P.S. My dearest, I love you "a real whole lot."
For always, I love you, Jackie

October 2, 1945
Tuesday night

Dearest husband,

I am happy tonight. Today I received loads of mail. Cill sent me three envelopes full, and Mrs. Gladden's son stopped in with another bunch. He was making a trip to Massachusetts and stopped in, but I wasn't home. There were eighteen V mails and one regular letter from September 15 to 21. Do you wonder now how I feel?

It is rather cool here. I went to two classes tonight, <u>Marketing</u> and <u>Journalism</u>, and enjoyed both. I am very well.

Shame on you, darling, for being late for church. In one letter you asked several questions about Phil and Bea. Well, you know the answers now. Yes, my getting ready to come to NY did remind me of that first summer with you. I don't mind though, as there is nothing that I like better than hopping on a train and going somewhere. I suppose it's the wanderlust in me. To tell the truth, dear, I haven't even been to have my picture taken yet. I hate having my picture taken. I will have to tell Mr. Gibson what you said about the write-up being good. A million thanks, darling, for the words of encouragement and good wishes for my success here. For knowing that you will be with me spiritually will mean everything in the world to me.

The snapshot, as usual, was very good, Phil—only you looked sort of sad and forlorn. Do you always look as nice over there as you do in the snapshots? You are doubtlessly a very well-dressed officer. It would be so nice to walk down the street beside you, Phil. I want to, so very, very much. I shall be waiting for the perfume. I hope Cill will send it to me. You know the way to my heart is through perfume, don't you?

When I read of Carpenter and the others coming home soon, I can't describe the feeling. It was awful, Phil. Then I thought of how much worse you must feel. It seems so unfair, but that's life, I suppose. And all of them have been with you so long! What about Overton? I hate to think of your being left behind while they come home. But maybe it won't be much longer for you. Sometimes I think about the fact that if I didn't love you and want you so terribly, that you would have been home ages ago, or maybe never have even gone over.

Yes, I remember that Sunday. We went to the park and read the papers. It was very hot. I recall too our eating at the automats and gaining "all that weight." I have learned, though, to lay off many of those things I used to like, such as mayonnaise, gravy, potatoes, macaroni, spaghetti, and bread. I still can't resist pie and cake and ice cream, though. Maybe with time, I can master my cravings for them too. Let's hope so anyway.

Phil, just as you, I too await for our first meeting. Sometimes, though I know I shouldn't, I permit myself to imagine how it might be, and I become afraid. I fear I might do something silly or ridiculous— though God forbid it. I don't want all these pent-up emotions, which I have held enslaved for going on three years, to burst from their fetters at one time. It must not be that way, dear. It would be maddening.

So you have ninety points now! Would that they could bring us together, dear! One sentence in your letter of two will always remain with me, Phil. It was "All of me with everything that is me and mine is yours."

About the thirty-eight points, that I was allowed. It will allow me to finish the course sooner. In several of your letters as of late, you have talked about bumping against me, "accidently or intentionally." Did you use to do it intentionally? I'm surprised at you.

In another letter, Phil, you said, "Every inch of me is you." That is as I want it to be always, darling.

Please keep well, darling, and don't despair, whatever happens. I know I've said that to you innumerable times, but I mean it now, just as much as I ever did.

Love, your wife,
Jack

P.S. I love you more than you know.

Notations on picture: Taken in France. Front row left to right: Milton, Scott, Kane, Armstead, Overton, Kurt (new company commander), Lawton Third row: Third from the left: Hurst

3 October 1945
Wednesday night
Part I only

My darling,

Today I received your special delivery letter telling me of your having found your apartment.

Sweets, I am glad. I know that you are feeling OK now. You can get settled, my sweetheart. Keep on being OK. You will, won't you? You must, dearest, because I want to feel swell all over.

My beloved, I know how you felt toward the Prince George Hotel. It's unusual that you were able to stay there as long as you did.

Sweetheart, I am glad that you like your classes. I hope they will continue to stay that way.

My darling, all of me will be yours as long as there is time and then after that. I'm per usual and all right.

Your husband,
Phil

P.S. My darling, I love you "a real whole lot." Always and forever.

4 October 1945
Thursday night
Part I only

My darling Jackie,

Dearest, today, I received a lot of mail again. I have letters from you for the nineteenth, twentieth, and twenty-fourth. They were all regular letters. Darling, you know how they made me feel, don't you? You're right, great all over. But just wait until I take you in my arms. Then I will be more than great. I will be feeling like a king all over.

My darling, I will write you a regular letter tonight. You won't mind, will you, sweet?

My sweetheart, you know all of me is still thoroughly and completely yours. Dearest, I won't ever change; if I do, I will be sure that it will be a change for the best. That's the truth, so help me, my Jackie.

My darling, I love you always.

Your husband,
Phil

P.S. My darling, I love you "a real whole lot." Always and forever yours.

7 October 1945
Sunday night
Part I only

My darling,

Today, as a Sunday, has passed like the rest. Lonely and empty. You know why, don't you? I'm without you, dearest. Honey, I miss you so much, I swear I do. Today has been a real Sunday. One in which we would have felt great just being together.

I as always hope that you are feeling great. I'm per usual and all right. I will stay that way for always. You know why, don't you, sweetheart? Yes, you're right, it's you alone.

I went to church this morning. I was not exactly on time. There were so many fellows there that I had to stand on the steps.

Dearest, I love you with all of me. I am yours, you know, through and through forever and through eternity. I am your eternal lover.

Your husband,
Phil

P.S. My darling, I love you "a real whole lot." Always and forever.

8 October 1945
Monday night
Part I (continued)

My darling Jackie,

Today, dearest, I received two of your letters. They were for the twenty-sixth and twenty-seventh of September. You know how they made me feel, don't you? That's it, great all over.

Darling, I'm glad that you are fine too. I'm glad that you are pleased with your new room.

You are right on the ball. You wouldn't find many people who would have cleaned that room like you did.

Darling, your description of the room you now have makes me want to come home as soon as possible. I know I'd like being there with you. I know I would, darling. I am positive of it.

Honey, don't you be straining yourself, carrying those heavy bags. Dear, I wish I could be near you to help you.

Your husband,
Phil

P.S. My darling, I love you "a real whole lot." Always, honest, I do, my dearest. Really, I do.

8 October 1945
Monday night
Part II (continued)

Dearest,

How dare you thinking how far the inner spring sink in for certain activities. Anyway, I'll be glad to be with you, Jackie, as soon as possible. You know, Mrs. Kane, I miss you too. I need you a terrible amount.

Dearest, I will be well all the time. I promise you that I will be thus always. I swear it, sweets.

This morning I had a real false alarm. They came to my bed, awakened me, and asked me if I wanted to go home. I said, "Hell, yes." OK, report now to an outfit which is leaving tomorrow. Reported to the outfit. My only mistake, I forgot to whitewash myself. I'm angry, mad, and some other things, but I'm still taking it on the chin. I'll be coming home though one of these days. I'll hit on the right thing.

Your husband,
Phil

P.S. My Jackie, I love you "a real whole lot." Always, truly, I'm yours, Jackie. Always too.

8 October 1945
Monday night
Part III (the end)

My beloved,

I'm praying that I will be home very soon. I want so very much to be with you, through and through.

Dear, I hope that you will have some mail coming to you soon, direct from me. That way, you won't have to depend on someone resending it.

This I do know, Jackie: it won't be very long before I am yours again. I am sure that it is only a matter of weeks now. Darling, keep your chin up. Be just as strong and brave as you have been all along. You've been my strength and my hope. I'll keep all keeps. Every one of them. I know naught else to do but to keep every one of them.

My dearest, I'm madly and completely yours. All of me.

Your husband,
Phil

P.S. My dearest, I love you "a real whole lot" Always and thoroughly, I'm your lover.

9 October 1945
Tuesday night
Part I only

My dearest beloved,

Today I received your letters for the twenty-eighth, twenty-ninth, and thirtieth of September. Darling, I feel great about them. They made my morale soar sky-high. Sweets, honest to goodness they are just what I needed even if I did receive two letters from you yesterday.

Sweetheart, I am going to write you a regular letter later tonight. That will be all right, won't it?

I am feeling fine, Jackie, per usual and all right. Dearest, I will stay that way. You know why, don't you, Jackie?

Today has been a fine one. One I'd love to spend with you, Jackie. I'm not kidding, that's the truth.

Darling, I love you. All of me belongs to you. Every part of me. Always and completely yours.

Your husband,
Phil

P.S. My darling, I love you "a real whole lot." Forever and always, I'm your Phil.

10 October 1945
Wednesday night
Part I only

My darling love,

Today has been a full day. Quite a full day. I have been in court all day. It was a rough session. I am fatigued, but not beat spiritually as I am sometimes. Also I had a lot of work to do in the company. Anyway, I can take it. Now, honey, don't worry about me because I'm in a way per usual and all right. And dearest, I am going to stay just right for you. Every part of me is just that way, my sweetheart.

My dumpling, I hope that you are as well as possible. I know you are.

My dearest, you know all of me is eternally yours. Dearest, I will never, ever change. My strength, heart, soul, mind, and body is completely yours.

All of me is your lover.

Your husband,
Phil

P.S. I love you "a real whole lot." Every infinitesimal part of does, Jackie darling.

11 October 1945
Thursday night
Part I only

My darling,

Today I received a letter from you for the first of October. It was as all your letters are. They are right on the ball. Dearest, I sure hope that the mail will get on the ball and hurry up and come to you. I know well how you feel, Jackie. I would be quite down in the boots if I did not get any mail.

Sweetheart, I'm sorry that you were tired and beat. Honey, I am pulling for you to be all right.

I am per usual and all right. As always, I will stay that way. I won't have it any other way.

Jackie, I miss you a great deal. I will continue to miss you too, my dearest. My beloved, all of me is completely yours.

Your husband,
Phil

P.S. My beloved, I love you "a real whole lot." Always and with all of me.

First Family Portrait: Phil, Jack and, daughter and book author, Jacqueline aka Lynne

Printed in the United States
By Bookmasters